Transforming Towns
Designing for Smaller Communities

RIBA  **Publishing**

Matthew Jones

© RIBA Publishing, 2020

Published by RIBA Publishing, 66 Portland Place, London, W1B 1AD

ISBN 978 1 85946 906 4

The right of Matthew Jones to be identified as the Author of this Work has been asserted in accordance with the Copyright, Designs and Patents Act 1988 sections 77 and 78.

British Library Cataloguing-in-Publication Data
A catalogue record for this book is available from the British Library.

Commissioning Editor: Alex White
Assistant Editor: Clare Holloway
Production: Sarah-Louise Deazley
Designed by Sarah-Louise Deazley
Typeset by Fakenham Prepress Solutions, Norfolk
Printed and bound by Page Bros, Norwich

While every effort has been made to check the accuracy and quality of the information given in this publication, neither the Author nor the Publisher accept any responsibility for the subsequent use of this information, for any errors or omissions that it may contain, or for any misunderstandings arising from it.

All quotes from external sources in the book were made in private correspondence with the author.

www.ribapublishing.com

CONTENTS

ACKNOWLEDGEMENTS

Many people have contributed to the research and practice that has led to the creation of this book over close to 15 years of thinking, practising and writing.

Without the help and support of the architects, design teams, clients and photographers behind the case studies who gave up their time to discuss their projects and provide their kind permission to use their photographs and images, this book would not have been possible.

The support, patience and understanding of RIBA Publishing throughout the publication process has been greatly appreciated, particularly the editorial advice of Alex White, Clare Holloway, those who reviewed the manuscript and Sarah-Louise Deazley for managing the production process.

Thank you to my PhD supervisor Professor Wayne Forster for his guidance and support in the development of my practice and PhD research and for contributing a Foreword to this book.

Thanks for their guidance, encouragement and valuable critique to my colleagues, friends, collaborators and students over the years at Birmingham School of Architecture and Design, Birmingham City University; the Department of Architecture and the Built Environment, the University of the West of England; Design Research Unit Wales, the Welsh School of Architecture; and Coombs Jones architects+makers. Collaboration with Design Commission for Wales and town councils and local authorities in Wales and the South West has also been valuable in developing the thinking behind parts of this work.

Last, but by no means least, I am profoundly thankful to my loving family, particularly Faye, Lily and Zachary, for their unending patience, inspiration and support. Without you none of this would have been possible. Thank you all.

ABOUT THE AUTHOR

Dr Matthew Jones is Associate Professor at the Birmingham School of Architecture and Design, Birmingham City University and a partner at Coombs Jones architects+makers. He is an architect whose practice, research and teaching have focused on place-specific approaches to the development of rural towns. Matthew led the award-winning Ruthin Future, a project to develop long-term vision for the future of the north Wales town. He has experience in socially engaged and participatory placemaking, community-led planning, public engagement and university-community live projects. Matthew was a judge for the RIBA President's Awards for Research 2017 and is an Advocate in Practice for Design Commission for Wales.

FOREWORD

Over the past two decades there has been a focus in architectural design on the city, the city region and more recently the rural. Special issues of well-known journals have been dedicated to these themes. The town – and small towns in particular – seem to have been squeezed out since the influential townscape movement of a half century ago, but as recent elections results revealed, ignore them at your peril.

For in Europe as a whole, small towns are home to one-fifth of the population. Beyond the broad metropolitan core regions of Europe the figure is often closer to one-third, as is the case in Wales and parts of England.

The majority of small towns were established as traditional market towns. Bypassed by the transport infrastructure – the motorway in particular – and stripped of their rail connections, these towns are remote from the economic motor regions. As *Free Market*, the Irish National Pavilion at the 16th International Architecture Exhibition La Biennale di Venezia 2018 which won widespread acclaim for its exploration of the unique identity of Irish towns, points out, 'out-migration has typically accounted for a disproportionate share of the brightest, most energetic, and best-educated young people, leaving aging populations that tend to become provincial and parochial in outlook. With declining economies and limited capacity to manage change, problems of economic, social and environmental problems become chronic.'[1] Their identity and distinctive sense of place is under threat and vulnerable to decline both in their social and built structure.

The most successful towns have capitalised on the significance to people of the local dimensions of liveability and quality of life. Building on local strengths, skills and resources, and painstakingly mapping and drawing out local distinctiveness, they feature niche product markets, local food chains and independent retail networks. However, even the most apparently affluent small towns face challenges of economic, cultural and environmental sustainability.

What can architecture offer? Because of the scale of towns even the most modest interventions can reinforce the settings in which life is lived and enjoyed. More strategically, the decision may be of what to build – or perhaps more crucially what not to build – and how to set the longer-term agenda that ensures historical and cultural continuity. Iconic thinking over iconic architecture.

The projects described in this book illustrate how good contemporary architecture can support and in some cases act as catalysts that strengthen and transform the identities of places. They also showcase the variety and diversity of skills, talents and determination that underpin the different forms of critical practice needed to uncover and reveal the value of good civic architecture to small towns.

The existing socio-economic gulf that exists between cities and towns may be said to be mirrored architecturally. As the gaze inevitably turns towards our towns and the estimated 9m people who dwell in them, the examples given in this book form a much needed and timely resource for all.

Professor Wayne Forster
Welsh School of Architecture,
Cardiff University

INTRODUCTION

Travel out of any British city and it is not long before you find yourself in one of the hundreds of small towns and villages that epitomise country life in the popular imagination – extraordinary places shaped by the nuances of their landscape, resources, growth and economy, steeped in history, rich in character and with a strong sense of community and pride. From medieval market towns to manufacturing centres, coastal villages, farming communities and picturesque tourist destinations, no two places are the same and their variety is one of their strengths. However, with the range of challenges facing small settlements, their fortunes vary dramatically. While some have experienced growth and prosperity, others have stagnated or atrophied following decline in industry and the rural economy. In order to survive and thrive, change is inevitable.

While often desirable and attractive places for residents and visitors, this idyllic vision of country life often conceals the range of challenges faced by many smaller communities. During the twentieth century their fortunes were radically altered by shifting rural employment patterns, increased car ownership, changing patterns of trade and consumption, and a rapid growth in communication technology. Improved transport connections opened many small towns to commuters drawn from urban environments by the prospect of a slower pace of life and a greater sense of community. Some places have grown dramatically to accommodate this demand and find themselves engulfed by sprawling low-density housing, industrial parks and retail estates. Drawing people away from town centres, these developments erode community cohesion and public life and increase reliance on the car. Other places have experienced a period of stagnation caused by a long-term decline in the rural economy and loss of industry and need to adapt to survive. The character and sense of place at the heart of the popularity of rural towns as places to live, work and play is under threat. For successful settlements, the challenge may be in managing growth and creating new places; for others, the best option may be to effectively control decline.

Throughout my studies and practice life these issues have been a growing concern. At the Welsh School of Architecture at Cardiff University, the design of sustainable, place-specific architecture was threaded through my student experience. Working at the Design Research Unit Wales (DRUw) after graduating, I was involved in projects exploring well-crafted contemporary architecture that learned from and enhanced its context, reinforcing local distinctiveness. We were inspired by architecture seen in small, often rural, communities in the Graubünden in Switzerland, the Vorarlberg in Austria and closer to home in Ireland and Scotland. I became concerned with how we as architects and designers could contribute more widely to the conversation about the future of these smaller places – places that often seemed overlooked by the profession. As part of my PhD research I was fortunate enough to visit two exemplars of long-term collaboration between an architect and a community, both in Switzerland: Gion Caminada's sensitive additions to the mountain village of Vrin in Graubünden and Luigi Snozzi's long-term collaboration with the community of Monte Carasso in the Ticino. These projects demonstrate how contemporary architecture can support and enrich a community and help it fulfil its long-term potential. This led me to consider comparable places I knew in the UK, but I found few examples of similar architect-community collaborations. High-quality contemporary architecture in small settlements in the UK remains under the radar. Where are these projects and what can we learn from them? How can we take a greater role in small communities to create projects that enhance distinctiveness and positively transform their place?

In writing this book I hope to investigate these questions, exploring how contemporary architecture can transform small communities across the UK and beyond. It describes the complex challenges faced by smaller communities and how these can be overcome through creativity, collaboration and long-term stewardship. High-quality architecture can learn from its context and feel rooted in its place without imitating what has gone before. It can embody a sense of continuity but it can also drive evolution, shifting the narrative from 'conserving' or 'preserving' to 'rethinking', 'championing' and 'transforming' small settlements. The case studies in this book are intended as a valuable resource offering both inspiration and the design guidance required to achieve this aspiration. Highlighting key lessons and design principles from each case study, it gives practitioners the tools to take the lead in creating positive futures for our small communities.

CHAPTER 1

Understanding Small Settlements

1.1 WHAT DO WE MEAN BY TOWNS AND SMALLER COMMUNITIES?

A fifth of the population of Europe lives in towns of under 50,000 people.[1] In many cases, these towns and small settlements have a high historical and cultural value but their growing desirability as places to live conceals challenges of decreasing distinctiveness and loss of vitality and culture.

The focus of this book is of these towns and smaller communities across the UK. There is no single definition in use but what is usually being referred to is one of the many settlements outside cities acting as a focus for rural life. Population also plays a role; the Centre for Towns identifies small towns, communities and villages as having a population of fewer than 30,000 people.[2] Their scale and population can leave them in an awkward 'in-between' position; they are places where urban and rural challenges collide but they often fall between policies aimed at the urban or the rural, gaining few of the benefits of either.

While this definition offers a focus, it does not consider the features and characteristics of smaller settlements that make them attractive to visitors and inhabitants and contribute to their sense of distinctiveness. The following section will explore this in more detail by examining the historic growth and contemporary pressures on smaller settlements.

1.2 HISTORY, GROWTH AND EVOLUTION

Prior to the completion of the Domesday Book in 1086 there were less than 50 urban places in England and Wales; by the fourteenth century this number had risen to over 500.[3] The majority developed as trading posts whose main reason for existence lay in the trading activities of the local hinterland.[4] Founded at strategic locations along routeways, fords, crossing points, safe harbours and near natural resources or at defensible positions,[5] the simple rule of a day's walk to market, a distance of around 10 km, helped establish a network of market towns linked into pan-European trading routes.[6] The focus for trade and exchange was the market square, the beating heart of town life. Some towns developed specialist markets and trades which grew to dominate their economy. For example, Beccles in Suffolk specialised in fish, Thaxted in Essex in knives, Ludlow in Shropshire in cloth and gloves, and Bridport in Dorset in robes.[7] This phase of growth between the eleventh and fourteenth centuries saw the foundation and growth of many of the places that have come to typify historic towns in the public imagination.

The sixteenth and seventeenth centuries brought new industries and buildings in the form of assembly rooms, pleasure gardens and covered market halls. During the eighteenth and nineteenth centuries, some settlements grew as small-scale manufacturing centres benefitting from connection into the rapidly expanding network of turnpikes, canals and railways. Mill towns, manufacturing towns, mining towns, brewing towns and railway towns proliferated, each with their own architectural language. New building types, such as warehouses, mills, factories, workers' institutes, breweries, stations and libraries, were built in their numbers. While some places prospered, others were bypassed by industrialisation and stagnated. By the late industrial period many smaller settlements were struggling to remain competitive in an increasingly city-centric and global world.

The twentieth century saw further radical alteration to the rural landscape. Changing patterns of agriculture and employment had dramatic consequences for smaller communities. Many livestock markets, previously intrinsic in the life of many towns, moved to the periphery or out of towns altogether. Town centres became dominated by retail and commercial functions rather than multifunctional places in which to reside, trade and socialise. With the boom in car ownership and vast improvements in infrastructure, the tightknit bonds between town and hinterland were disrupted and people could live, work and shop further afield. New roads caused radical change to the form of some towns and encouraged growth of new housing, employment and industry in peripheral locations. Mono-functional estates and retail nodes along distributor and ring roads skirted town cores. The compact nature of historic settlements was largely rejected in favour of low-density, car-centred peripheral development. Many towns have lost their coherence and legibility; the sense of place at the heart of their popularity as places to live, work and play is under threat.

1.3 CONTEMPORARY CHALLENGES FACING SMALLER COMMUNITIES

THE CHANGING ROLES OF SMALL SETTLEMENTS

Traditionally, small settlements were the focus of agricultural and manufacturing trading activity of the countryside, existing in a 'symbiotic relationship'[8] with their surrounding area. Over the past two centuries smaller settlements have faced radical and rapid change and today the picture is complex. The shifting nature of the global economy has dramatically altered the function of rural places and their relationships with city, nation and world. They have a diverse range of roles and functions beyond the traditional service centre role (see Table 1.1).

Service centres	The traditional 'market town' role of a town offering services to the hinterland.
Visitor attractions	Often remote from urban areas or close to areas of natural beauty, national parks or coastlines.
Locations for specialised employment	Settlements dominated by one employer, such as the military or manufacturing, often characterised by young populations.
Commuter towns	Settlements attracting residents seeking a small-town 'lifestyle'. Many have good transport links to allow easy travel to urban centres.
Housing the retired	Attractive market towns are often popular locations for retirement due to their perceived slow way of life, impacting on house prices and demand for services.

Table 1.1 Five functional roles of towns as described by Powe, Hart and Shaw[9]

The continuing success of small settlements is affected by proximity to larger towns and cities, patterns of travel and public transport, local authority and regional boundaries, local employment, availability of public services and attractiveness to tourism.[10] For some settlements, decades of stagnation have led to out-migration, ageing populations, apathy and a limited capacity to affect change.[11] Elsewhere, other settlements are thriving as a perceived higher quality of life attracts an ever increasing number of people to live in rural areas.[12]

While positive for local businesses and services, increased demand for rural housing can inflate house prices and exacerbate shortages of affordable housing. Peripheral housing estates, poorly connected to existing settlements and with increasing reliance on the car,[13] accommodate incomers but contribute little to distinctiveness and community.

ENHANCING CHARACTER AND DISTINCTIVENESS
Recent development and planning policy has often failed to engage with the place-specific conditions that make small settlements unique. For many people, historic buildings and townscapes are a vital component of the character of small settlements and one of the key factors in their distinctiveness. No two places are the same. The character of a town or village has been shaped by centuries of history and the specifics of the regional cultural landscape: its climate, topography, local materials, agriculture and industry. This cumulative legacy affects the look and feel of a place and shapes how people perceive and respond to their surroundings.[14] In order to preserve the character of sensitive historic centres, many are protected through conservation areas, while important buildings are protected through listing. However, the additional challenges of working in these sensitive

contexts can deter development. The perceived additional cost and difficulty in adapting listed buildings, limited plot sizes, potential for conflict with local people and an additional layer of regulations can limit redevelopment in historic centres. Empty, derelict or dilapidated buildings can create negative perceptions and perpetuate town centre decline.

Gaining an understanding of how a place has been affected by historic factors is vital in considering its future, generating support from the local community and developing the next layer of their evolution. Under the UK government National Planning Policy Framework (NPPF), planning policies should aim to connect people and place, integrating new developments into their natural, historic and built environments.[15]

The difficult task of achieving this in smaller communities has undergone limited research. In 2002 a study by the Commission for Architecture and the Built Environment (CABE) and English Heritage highlighted 15 best practice exemplars of new buildings integrated into historic contexts.[16] The report illustrates a range of responses to context from neo-vernacular to a contemporary architectural language. It demonstrates that new buildings can be successfully integrated into historic contexts and recommends collaboration, careful study of context, use of traditional materials in a contemporary way and high environmental standards as a basis for successful design in historic settings. The report further outlines clear indicators of compromise – stepping down as a new building meets a neighbour, application of historic elements out of context, replicating materials (for example, panellised brickwork) and the reuse of motifs from small-scale vernacular buildings on larger buildings, resulting in a pastiche.[17] More recent guidance for designing new architecture to enhance local distinctiveness and generate support from the local community is currently lacking, and recent best practice examples are few and far between.

THE DECLINE OF TOWN CENTRES AND HIGH STREETS
The high street is a vital part of many people's perception of the places in which they live, work and spend their leisure time. Their physical quality, social activity and offer of goods and services are an important part of people's sense of belonging.[18] However, the role of the market and traditional high street as a focus for trade and commerce is diminishing, the result of a long-term shift from production to consumption. The growth of out-of-town retail outlets and supermarkets, combined with the boom in online shopping, are changing patterns of retail. This is having a tangible impact on town centres. One in 12 shops has closed over the past five years.[19] Visits to town centres are down 17% over the past decade, impacted by the 4.65 m² of out of town retail built between 2000 and 2009.[20] Banks, post offices, health services

and schools have faced drastic cuts and sweeping closures. Many public bodies are consolidating assets to larger settlements, reducing the service provision that brings people to town and village centres. While in cities and large towns the closure of smaller branches may be inconvenient, there will often be other options available. In communities with a much smaller population there are often no other alternatives and residents are left without essential services.

The quality and diversity of high streets and town centres has a major impact on the perception of residents and visitors. In a survey of over 160 towns, villages and neighbourhoods carried out by the New Economics Foundation, 41% were identified as 'clone towns', places dominated by generic and near-identical high street shopping chains found across the country. The report further indicates that 36% were characterised as 'home towns', places that retained an individual character that could be instantly recognised by inhabitants and visitors.[21] This sense of character and distinctiveness is important in attracting local people and visitors to use town centres. Negative perceptions can be reversed through creatively reimagining what and who town centres and high streets are for and developing their purpose beyond retail alone. Making good use of heritage assets, creating attractive town centres, rethinking the purpose of empty shops, encouraging a lively atmosphere through events and activities, considering parking costs and creating a safe and attractive public realm that encourages people to walk, linger and socialise can revitalise ailing town centres. Through imagination, innovation and effective involvement of local people, inspiring strategies that draw on changing patterns of living, working and playing can catalyse positive change.

PERIPHERAL GROWTH
In contrast to town centre locations, peripheral locations offer opportunities where there are fewer restrictions on design, scale, access, parking and plot size. Since the twentieth century, mono-functional urban extensions characterised by standardised low-density design have proliferated. Often poorly connected to town centres and local services, they increase reliance on the car.[22] These anonymous estates of housing, retail, business parks and industry have scant response to place and do little to encourage community.

Accommodating housing need is a particularly important issue. Small settlements face a range of housing pressures depending on their location and role. For some, loss of population, especially younger residents, leaves an ageing population often poorly catered for in the housing market. Others attract 'counter-urbanisers' from cities who compete with local people for housing, raising house prices. Improved mobility has been instrumental in this shift; those living in rural areas accept longer commuting times in order to combine levels of income associated with employment in cities with the lifestyle benefits of rural living.[23]

In order to accommodate new homes, mono-functional urban extensions characterised by standardised low-density homes have proliferated since the mid-twentieth century. Often aimed at the commuter market where travel to work, school, shop and play is ingrained in everyday life, these edge developments can be seen to be at an advantage against town cores, with affordable prices and easy access to ring roads and bypasses.[24] In their low density, excessive land consumption and lack of integration with existing communities, these suburban estates do little to enhance distinctiveness or encourage community (see Figures 1.1 and 1.2). In the longer term it is often these newcomers who oppose new development and advocate for the status quo.[25]

1.1 A dense urban core surrounds the market place, Richmond, Yorkshire

1.2 Identikit housing proliferates around popular towns

There are positive examples of new development and urban extensions integrating successfully into existing settlements with the support of local people and becoming part of the life of their community. Understanding local character and patterns of development over time and seeing new development as an evolution of these traditions helps embed new development in its place. Allowing public access and creating new links for pedestrians and cyclists can knit new development into existing travel networks. New homes should consider what people need today and into the future, incorporating the lifestyles and desires of different demographics and meeting changing performance requirements. To be effective, local people need to be part of the process of thinking about the future of their place, and the people who know their places are best engaged throughout.

NURTURING SOCIAL LIFE

Beyond the character of built form, social life is vital in creating thriving communities. Public spaces – squares, streets and lanes – are essential components of the everyday life of small settlements, providing an important social space for meeting and encounter, a place where the familiar and unexpected collide.[26] The function of many town squares changes with the seasons and time of day. The location of markets, festivals, events and the town Christmas tree, squares continue to be the centre of town life. In small communities, it could be argued that with fewer and potentially more dispersed people, social engagement needs to be fostered more than in cities; thereby creating opportunities for social exchange is critical.[27]

Well-designed and maintained streetscapes and spaces have a positive economic impact, increasing footfall within town centres. This, in turn, has a beneficial social impact, increasing conviviality through events, accidental meeting and socialising, as well as health benefits, encouraging people to spend time outdoors (see Figures 1.3 and 1.4). However, in many streets and squares in smaller settlements, movement, events, parking, pedestrians, vehicles, shops, cafés, monuments, trees, seating and lighting all compete for space, resulting in confusing and contradictory spaces. By trying to cater for so many uses, these spaces can end up being ideal for none and the sense of street life and conviviality needed to support the social life of smaller communities can be lost.

High-quality spaces are more likely to be well used and encourage people to stay. Many small places have networks of public space threaded through their fabric which are used in different ways. How well these spaces connect and the quality of the spatial experience moving through and between them affects people's perception of a place. Creating opportunities for inhabitation and chance encounter encourages people to linger and interact socially. Attention to small details, such as historic shop frontages, unified street furniture and material qualities, can enhance the character of public space. Simple moves such as reducing street clutter, balancing priority between vehicles and pedestrians or improving long term maintenance and upkeep can dramatically affect the feel of a place. Often, small scale or incremental change can have a significant impact in creating places for people to inhabit and enjoy.

1.3 Informal public spaces create opportunities for accidental meeting and social interaction, Ludlow, Shropshire

1.4 A formal market Square, Alnwick, Northumberland

Understanding Small Settlements **13**

FROM CHALLENGES TO OPPORTUNITIES?

There have been a number of recent attempts to encourage long-term thinking in delivering change in small communities. However, despite the value of sustained, long-term, design-led engagement in transforming settlements, not enough is being done. Many well-intentioned ideas, reports, visions and masterplans are short-lived or end up collecting dust on a council office shelf, whereas what small towns require is sustained, long-term and place-sensitive processes.[28] Despite this, there is a significant opportunity to renew existing settlements, create new sustainable neighbourhoods to accommodate housing growth, generate new visions for town centres and encourage a sense of community cohesion. If the approach is 'business as usual' and development happens with little thought for distinctiveness, place or community, there is a risk that the result will be yet more anonymous retail and suburban housing growth, extending and engulfing settlements. Overcoming these challenges has significant consequences for how we as designers conceive the urban environment and the skills we can contribute to rethinking and championing small settlements.

1.4 TIME FOR CHANGE

The fortunes of small settlements are changing. The political eye is shifting and funds are becoming available to catalyse development. The UK government recently pledged to reduce business rates with the aim to support small businesses, and in 2019 it launched two programmes: the £1.6 billion Stronger Towns Fund to boost economic growth in towns and the Future High Streets Fund to reverse the fortunes of ailing high streets. In early 2020, the Welsh government announced a £90 million fund to support a 'town centre first' approach, building on nearly £800 million invested since 2014. Scotland's Towns Partnership, a collaborative forum for towns, supports and disseminates best practice and provides data and analysis tools for communities and designers. The Charette process, an inclusive participatory planning method funded by the Scottish government since 2011, has so far been carried out in over 48 communities, many of them towns and villages.[29] The Scottish Government Town Centre Fund, established in 2019, aims to provide place-based investment to enable town centres to re-purpose, diversify and flourish. *Free Market*, the Irish National Pavilion at the 16th International Architecture Exhibition at the 2018 Venice Biennale, focused on the importance of the common spaces of Ireland's market towns and subsequently toured the country exploring ideas and dreams for their future.[30]

With smaller communities becoming a focus for policy, now is the time for us to take the lead in championing smaller communities. Architects and designers can play a vital role in transforming their futures and creating thriving places.

The following chapters demonstrate the transformative potential architects and designers can have working in smaller settlements. The projects span a range of scales and typologies and demonstrate successful integration of contemporary architecture into sensitive settings and the creation of distinctive places. These are innovative approaches to urban intensification and the creation of new sustainable neighbourhoods that show a considered, careful response to character, create new forms of living and enhance feelings of belonging. New models of public building can support the cultural life of towns and villages, from cultural buildings with a civic role to re-thinking the provision of local governance and services. High-quality public spaces can help social life to flourish, supporting the rhythms and rituals of everyday life. Long-term projects can create positive change through sustained creative engagement with local people and groups and imaginative, realisable visions to deliver effective long-term transformation.

With skills in problem-solving, mediating disparate views and collaborative working and creative design, architects are well-placed to take the lead in considering change in our towns and villages. Now is the time for us to take charge of the debate, champion our smaller settlements and deliver positive change in small towns and villages.

CHAPTER 2

Homes: Creating Distinctive Places to Live

2.1 THE NEED FOR NEW HOMES

Housing delivery is near the top of today's political agenda. There is a crisis of increasing homelessness, falling rates of home ownership and of affordability of both homes for rental and for purchase. The often-cited solution to address these multiple crises is to build more homes, faster. To keep up with housing demand we need to build between 240,000 and 340,000 new homes per year,[1] the majority of which will be in or around existing settlements. The recently revised National Planning Policy Framework (NPPF) promotes new housing development and aims to increase housing densities on developable land. If these aims are to be met, many small settlements will undergo considerable housing expansion, with some predicted to expand by up to 25%.[2] However, the challenge goes beyond numbers; we need the right homes, in the right place, at the right price, for the right people. Demand must be balanced with high-quality, sustainable homes which respond to local character.

The case studies in this chapter illustrate how new village and town housing can draw inspiration from local character and context to create distinctive places in which to live. From small-scale infill development on brownfield sites to larger urban extensions, they demonstrate how imaginative and contemporary new homes can be designed to respond to local character, integrate into existing settlements and expand housing provision to suit contemporary lifestyles.

HOUSING PRESSURES ON SMALL COMMUNITIES

Since the mid-twentieth century many small settlements have seen considerable housing growth. The increased availability of cheap motoring has been instrumental in this shift. For some places a perceived higher quality of life attracts 'counter-urbanisers' from cities to nearby rural areas, drawn by more spacious and often cheaper housing and an aspiration for the perceived qualities of the 'country life'. This desirability can drive up house prices; on average house prices are 25% higher than in urban areas while wages are lower.[3] Local people, and in particular younger residents, can become excluded from accessing the housing market. This is further exacerbated by a shrinking stock of rural social homes available for local people.[4]

At the same time, many smaller settlements have increasingly ageing populations. Within five years the over-sixties will constitute 25% of the English population who are statistically more likely to reside in, or wish to move to, small towns and villages.[5] However, this demographic is often poorly catered for in the housing market in smaller settlements. The recent HAPPI 4 (Housing our Ageing Population: Panel for Innovation) report identified the need to provide more purpose-built accommodation for older people in rural areas. It recommended that while specialist housing, such as extra care and assisted living, may be located in towns for economies of scale, smaller-scale developments for those 'right sizing' from owner-occupied homes, agricultural dwellings and social housing no longer suited to their needs could be provided for locally to help preserve independence and care needs.[6]

ACCOMMODATING GROWTH

In many places, the response to housing demand has been the growth of low-density housing estates around the edges of historic centres. Served by new roads and bypasses, mono-functional urban extensions characterised by standardised homes turn their backs on existing settlements and have limited response to context. Poor pedestrian and cycle connections isolate residents from the wider community and increase dependence on the car. While built-up historic centres can have a density of up to 475 dwellings per hectare, low-density suburban estates can be as low as eight dwellings per hectare.[7] Although new housing has a role in supporting local services and retail, evidence suggests that there are low levels of engagement with local services from in-migrants living in peripheral locations.[8] There is a risk that this pattern of development will continue in the drive to deliver housing numbers over the creation of high quality, well-connected places people want to live.

2.1.0 A new build housing estate on the edge of Frome, Somerset

2.1.1 A new build housing estate in Ludlow, Shropshire, shares many similarities with the example in Frome

There is significant potential to integrate new housing into existing settlements. The Campaign to Protect Rural England (CPRE) has identified the potential for over 1 million new homes on brownfield sites across the UK.[9] Small settlements are no exception, and vacant and backland sites offer plenty of potential to intensify existing settlements. These sites are often complex but offer the opportunity to integrate new homes within existing urban fabric close to shops, services, schools, employment and outdoor spaces. Sites on the edges pose different challenges. Here, connection to, and integration with, existing settlements is vital to ensure new homes contribute to the continuity and distinctiveness of a place.

DELIVERING LOCALLY DISTINCTIVE HOMES

The revised NPPF (2018) promotes new housing development and an increase in housing densities while advocating homes with 'local distinctiveness'. The positive value of distinctive contemporary housing has been championed by the RIBA, most recently through the report 'Ten Characteristics of Places where People want to Live' (2018), developed to inform the profession and wider industry of the importance of design quality and placemaking in the delivery of new homes. The report highlighted the need for clear leadership, collaboration between public and private sector, engaging the wider community and innovating in the design process to deliver new places where people want to live.[10]

Four architecture practices – Pollard Thomas Edwards (PTE), HTA Design LLP, Proctor & Matthews and PRP Architects – also produced 'Distinctively Local' (2019), a report focusing on what good quality aspirational design informed by local character looks like. It describes four key attributes:

1. Response to context.

2. People-friendly spaces and streets.

3. Crafting houses that feel like home.

4. Providing choice and diversity.[11]

These reports highlight examples of new homes embodying the aspiration for local distinctiveness, but they are in the minority. In many other cases superficial references to local building forms or vernacular materials applied to standardised house plans suffice to gain planning consent.[12] This is not a genuine response to context and often results in a product that neither has support from local people nor suits the needs of contemporary lifestyles.

The role of the architect should be to interpret historic patterns to inform contemporary design solutions that evolve local traditions while responding to the needs of twenty-first-century living. The challenge of designing homes with the right balance of traditional and contemporary should begin with a thorough analysis of the local contexts – physical, social and historical – to inform the pattern of development. Decisions of scale, mass, volume, grain and form should relate to the character of the locale. It may start early in the design process with consideration of topography, landscape and urban fabric. Understanding the boundaries between areas of a settlement or where it meets surrounding countryside can help integrate new development and prevent sprawl. In larger developments, creating character areas with distinctive features, scale, forms or materials can create a sense of identity.

Using historic maps to understand typical features of smaller settlements, such as long, thin burgage plots, terraced housing for workers, clusters of farm buildings or patterns of fields or walls can provide clues for designers.[13] Inspiration can be found in roof forms, shop frontages, details, thresholds, entrances or use of colour to inform emerging design ideas. Consideration of the networks and patterns of movement in the surrounding streets, lanes, paths and green spaces for pedestrians, cyclists and vehicles can help connect new development into existing settlements and communities.

Architectural form and expression can be influenced by the local character and celebrate its peculiarities to embed new development in its place. However, historic patterns should not be merely recorded and repeated. New homes need to suit contemporary needs and lifestyles and meet shifting performance requirements. Through understanding and reinterpretation of patterns, scale, material, connections and colour, new development can be imbued with a strong sense of distinctiveness and identity, evolving traditions to meet twenty-first century needs.

The following projects demonstrate innovative approaches to urban intensification and the creation of new sustainable neighbourhoods that show a considered, careful response to character, create new forms of living and enhance belonging. From a small-scale development of nine homes bringing new life to a derelict pub to 76 new homes connecting a series of character areas in the heart of a historic market town, these projects demonstrate the potential of new homes to respond to the character of their context while remaining distinctly contemporary.

Location: Temple Cloud, Somerset, UK

Population: 1,300

Number of homes: 9

Contract value: Confidential

Status: Completed 2017

Community pubs, one of the oldest and most popular of UK social institutions, are under considerable pressure. More than a quarter of pubs in the UK have closed since 2001, with the biggest decline seen outside cities.[14] In smaller towns and villages, pubs are an important focus of village life, providing places where a community can 'bounce off itself' – not just for socialising but also for hosting activities, groups, meetings and clubs which contribute to civic life.[15] In Temple Cloud, the transformation of a failing country pub has created new homes in the heart of the village and has provided a renewed focus for community life, sustaining a valuable village institution for the future.

2.2.0 The new homes seen through the central courtyard

SITE AND CONTEXT

Temple Cloud is a small village located on the A37, a historic turnpike and busy thoroughfare to the south of Bristol and Bath. The Grade II listed Temple Inn is located on a 0.34-ha site at an important junction in the heart of the village. Its Georgian façade fronts a junction with a garden, car park, a barn used as a skittle alley and an area of scrubland behind. The last remaining pub in the village, the Temple Inn had struggled to survive, and a new approach was needed to ensure the long-term future of this important site at the centre of the community.

The development arm of Red Oak Taverns, Bath & Stratford Homes, has brought numerous unloved and failing pubs back to life through a programme of capital investment and improved management. Following the purchase of the Temple Inn from liquidators in 2012, the architectural practice Archio was commissioned to develop a scheme for the renovation of the pub and the surrounding site. By securing the long-term future of the pub and providing new homes in its centre, the aim was to re-establish the site as part of the fabric and life of the village. The resulting project consists of the refurbished Temple Inn, a new building containing 10 guest rooms for the pub and nine three- and four-bed houses for market sale (*see* Figure 2.2.1).

2.2.1 The addition of three new buildings framing the Temple Inn in housing allow it to become integrated into the fabric of the village once again

INTERPRETING THE VILLAGE CHARACTER

Archio's starting point was an investigation of the village: its growth, development and distinctive features. The existing pattern of the village is characterised by groupings of buildings in informal clusters which over time have merged as the village has densified. These clusters consist of rows of cottages with small front gardens accessed by shared pathways with areas of open space – yards, parking courts or informal green spaces – at their heart. Temple Gardens responds to these characteristics, creating a new cluster around the existing pub and barn. New buildings are arranged in terraces to create two yards. An informal cluster of buildings look out onto a shared green space that acts as a focal point for the homes, which is separated from a second yard providing car parking for the pub (see Figures 2.2.2 and 2.2.3). Views through the site to the wider village and countryside beyond link the development to its village context.

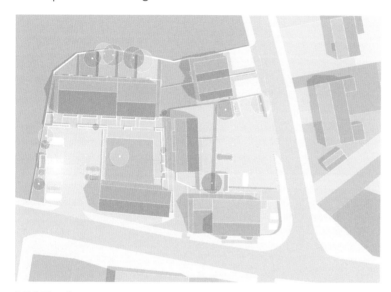

2.2.2 Site plan

2.2.3 A new terrace, converted barn and semi-detached homes are clustered around a green courtyard

The new homes are configured into a long terrace of five three- and four-bed homes facing the green, a pair of larger semi-detached homes accessed from a quieter side road and two homes located in the converted barn. Use of roof space as a third storey allows for some larger homes, while keeping the height of the buildings below the historic pub. Internally, the homes are compact but feel generous thanks to 2.5-m ceiling heights and large windows providing high levels of daylighting and a sense of space. Staircases are roof-lit, dropping light into the centre of the homes, while bedrooms in roof spaces with large dormer windows create an additional bedroom within a compact floor area. The letting rooms are located alongside the refurbished historic pub, providing a visual and acoustic barrier between the new homes and the busy A37. Internally, the letting rooms look out towards the central green space, buffered from the street by an access corridor.

CREATING THRESHOLDS

Access and parking are carefully considered and located so as not to dominate the central green space. Resident parking is restricted to a gravel parking court to the north of the letting rooms while the larger semi-detached houses to the south have individual driveways. A shared pathway flanked by planters and benches provides access to the new homes. Recessed porches and small, hedged front gardens create a deep threshold with a layer of semi-private, defensible space. Brick planters outside front windows provide a second layer of privacy between private kitchens and living rooms and the central green.

INTERPRETING LOCAL MATERIALS AND DETAILS

The new homes draw from the Somerset vernacular to inform their form, material and detail. A careful study of local buildings and typologies led to the development of details such as the stone window surrounds, dormer windows, asymmetric window positions and gables facing the road (see Figures 2.2.4 and 2.2.5).

2.2.4 Examples of gable-ended cottages found in the village

2.2.5 The two semi-detached houses with gables facing the street

Material reference is made to the existing pub, whose limestone façade is extended across the letting rooms, lending a sense of weight to the street façade. Elsewhere, brick is the predominant material – a reference to the former brickworks located opposite the site – with cast stone used for details such as oversize window surrounds and copings (see Figures 2.2.6 and 2.2.7). The tradition of stone window reveals in brick walls and brick reveals to rubble elevations, evident across the wider village, are interpreted in stretcher bond brick reveals to the windows in the lettable rooms and the expressed cast stone window surrounds used in the new homes. A sense of informality is created through the location of these surrounds, dormers breaking the roof line and by recessed front doors.

2.2.6 An example of a stone window surround in the village

2.2.7 Cast stone oversized window surrounds refer to examples in the village

CONCLUSION

Temple Gardens has transformed a derelict public house and rejuvenated it as a cornerstone of the local community by intensifying its site. New facilities for the pub, such as lettable rooms, sit alongside a series of contemporary homes in the heart of a sensitive village context. The development demonstrates how an understanding of historic patterns – seen here in the interpretation of clustered farm buildings around courtyards – can create a link between a new development and its context. While its material and detail draw inspiration from distinctive local features, it is reinvented using contemporary materials and forms in a development that feels both contemporary and contextual. Temple Gardens demonstrates how a relatively small development of new homes can be successfully integrated into a village setting, adding a new layer to the history of a place and creating a vibrant new social heart that enables the community to thrive.

TRANSFORMATIONS

- **Community and amenity**: regeneration of a community asset through considered investment which diversifies the use of the site and offers potential for a sustainable future for an important village amenity.

- **Character and sense of place**: the project demonstrates the value of in-depth study of the context to inform design decisions – particularly evident in the cluster form and material detailing – resulting in a careful knitting of the development into the fabric of the village.

- **Simple forms**: simple but contemporary forms informed by studies of the local vernacular have embedded the project in its place without pastiche.

- **Public space**: the clustered form with a shared green space at its heart extends the pattern of the village and offers potential for neighbourliness and social interaction.

- **Access and parking**: grouping parking spaces alongside the central green space minimises roadways and enables a generous shared central space to be created.

CREDITS

Architect: Archio

Developer: Bath and Stratford Homes

Contractor: Ken Biggs Contractors Ltd

Structural engineer: Entuitive

Quantity surveyor: Ward Williams Associates

Acoustic engineer: Acoustic

Interior design: Pembrook Design and Jane Clayton & Co.

Environmental / M&E engineer: One Creative Environments Ltd

Awards: RIBA South West Award 2018

Location: Rye, East Sussex, UK

Population: 4,773

Number of homes: 10 (six flats, two penthouses, one detached house and one studio)

Contract value: £2.3m

Status: Completed 2015

An infill development in the historic Cinque Ports town of Rye, this mixed-use project combines contemporary design in a conservation area with off-site manufacture to minimise disruption to the town centre during construction. With stripped-back detailing and elegant materials, the project creates a bold addition to the street, which interprets the traditional burgage plot to create a contemporary mix of houses and apartments in the heart of the town.

2.3.0 The project is located in Rye's historic heart

SITE AND CONTEXT

Rye is a fortified port town in East Sussex, located at the confluence of the Rother, Tillingham and Brede rivers. Along with Winchester, the town was one of the two 'ancient towns' of the Cinque Ports Confederation, bringing immense wealth and prosperity during the medieval period. A depth of history is embedded in its contemporary fabric; a rich mix of uses rub against each other in a blend of predominantly two- and three-storey medieval buildings with an abundance of finely crafted and quirky details. This new mixed-use development on a former industrial site, derelict since 2002, creates a contemporary addition to the heart of the town. Situated in the core of Rye's conservation area at the boundary of the medieval and the eighteenth-century towns, the site included the ruins of the medieval town wall, a scheduled ancient monument. The bold new development completes the street, infilling a brownfield site with a dense mix of apartments and houses, introducing new homes suited to contemporary lifestyles to the heart of the town.

ORGANISATION AND FORM

The project reinstates a street frontage to Cinque Ports Street. Two commercial units face the street with a mix of flats and penthouses above, accessed from a shared stairwell fronting the street. This streetside four-storey block has a formal simplicity with five bays differentiated by asymmetric roof forms, strongly evocative of the jumbled roofs visible across the town. A subtle stepping of the street façade, timber-clad above a render base, follows the surrounding building lines (see Figure 2.3.1).

2.3.1 The courtyard separating the streetside block from the mews houses behind

Behind the apartment block is a narrow central courtyard accessed through a passageway from the street. This is reminiscent of passages and yards in Rye's medieval fabric, an important aspect of the townscape character. Narrow alleys cut through the town, framing views of half-hidden buildings, streets or the landscape beyond. The courtyard separates the streetside apartment block from two smaller buildings behind, a two-storey house and a one-bedroom studio (see Figures 2.3.2 and 2.3.3). Smaller in size, their scale and form were designed to preserve light to surrounding

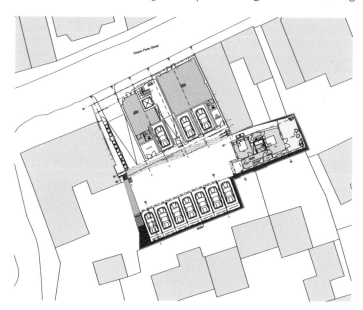

2.3.2 Ground floor plan

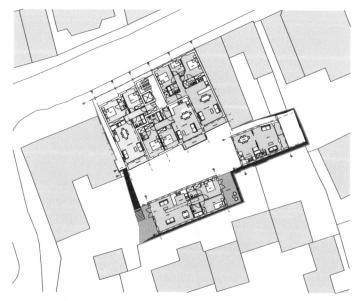

2.3.3 First floor plan

buildings. Façades facing into this shared central space are more open and informal. Large south-facing balconies overlook the courtyard, maximising light into the apartment living spaces and framing views out across the town, giving residents a sense of belonging to their wider community.

The courtyard doubles as vehicular access to garages and parking bays located beneath a raised apartment. Each home has one allocated parking space accessed via a ramp cutting through the streetside block. While this minimises the impact of the car, it perhaps compromises the extent to which the courtyard can be used as a shared communal space by residents.

FORMAL AND MATERIAL SIMPLICITY

The material palette draws from the surrounding context, in particular the timber-gabled, barn-like harbourside warehouses and coastal architecture found along the Sussex coastline. It is a contemporary take on the simple forms of local traditional architecture and emphasises the plot widths through a dramatic angular roof form and a stepping street façade. Dark-stained timber, slate and render are used throughout with pared-back detailing and treatment. Window frames and gutters are concealed to emphasise the simplicity of the form. Apparently randomly placed windows on the street façade continue the irregular rhythm of the surrounding buildings. The overall effect is of a sense of abstraction of the traditional forms and details of the town into a new architectural language that grows out of its place (see Figure 2.3.4).

2.3.4 The asymmetrical roof seen across the rooftops, an evolution of the language of the town

The same material palette continues in the courtyard. While the two mews-style houses are simple pitched roof forms designed to preserve light to surrounding properties, the rear of the streetside apartment building is more informal. A pushing and pulling of the building form is expressed in the timber lining of recessed balconies to the apartment living rooms and two extruded balconies clad in timber (see Figure 2.3.5). This treatment echoes historic burgage plot development patterns which typically have a formal and composed public front and more informal private yards and buildings behind. Views across the town are framed from within the shared stairwell, linking the residents to their setting and helping to develop a sense of belonging (see Figure 2.3.6).

2.3.5 Inset and projecting balconies face the courtyard

2.3.6 Views across the town are framed through large windows

CONCLUSION

Transforming a derelict industrial site, the stepping building form and irregular pitched roofs capture the character of the medieval town and respond to the neighbouring buildings. A central courtyard recalling the yards across the town allows light into the heart of the scheme and creates a focal stripped-back, minimal detailing, creating a distinctly contemporary interpretation of the town's architecture, resulting in a striking contemporary mixed-use scheme that strengthens the heart of the historic town and creates new opportunities for living in the town centre.

TRANSFORMATIONS

- **Character and sense of place**: a simple form which references the narrow burgage plots through the stepping façade and roof form links the building to its place while remaining contemporary.

- **Mixed use**: different sizes of home with ground floor commercial units demonstrate how a mix of new uses can be integrated into the heart of a historic town.

- **Simple forms**: pared-back detailing and simple materials emphasise the simplicity of the building massing, which is inspired by traditional building forms. Distorting these angular forms adds a sense of distinctiveness and drama to the street.

- **Central courtyard**: the building is organised around a hardworking courtyard which protects the historic town wall, allows access to undercroft parking and creates a shared space between the streetside and mews blocks.

CREDITS

Client: confidential

Architect: Jonathan Dunn Architects

Main contractor: Jenners

Structural engineer: J.M. Loades and Associates Ltd

Quantity surveyor: Paul Latham

M+E engineer: Reina Group

Archaeological surveyor: Chris Butler / South East Archaeological Society

Awards: RIBA South East Regional Award 2016

Location: Southwold, Suffolk, UK

Population: 1,098

Number of homes: 38 (16 apartments and 12 houses for sale, 10 affordable homes)

Contract value: £6.5m

Status: Completed 2011

Addressing a pressing need for affordable homes in the heart of Southwold, Tibby's Triangle carefully weaves new homes into an existing historic fabric. Through an intimate network of new streets, lanes, yards and alleyways, a formerly industrial site is opened up to the town. Knitting into the town's fabric, the project demonstrates how an in-depth awareness of the intricacies of the town's history and urban grain can influence the design of rich and characterful places in which to live.

2.4.0 Drayman Square, the heart of the development

SITE AND CONTEXT

Southwold is an unspoilt seaside town on the Suffolk Heritage coast popular with summer tourists. The lighthouse, the flint tower of St Edmund's Church and Adnams Brewery – the town's largest single employer – dominate the skyline of the town. Its fabric is characterised by a mixed architecture connected by a network of alleys, greens, yards and gardens. The town has little post-war development of any kind; with exponential growth of second homes and holiday lets, Southwold has seen house prices soar and local people forced out of the housing market. This has resulted in a declining adult population and has particularly affected families and young people who struggle to find housing to suit their needs in the town. In 2006, Southwold Council identified a strategy for more affordable housing to address this need, a principle at the heart of the Tibby's Triangle development.

The 0.4-ha site, located next to the Grade I listed St Edmund's Church and close to the beach, became available after the decision by Adnams to move its distribution centre to the edge of the town. Sited immediately off the high street, it offered the opportunity to address housing need within the conservation area at the heart of the town. Following an invited design competition, Ash Sakula was appointed to develop proposals for a wine and kitchen store for Adnams and a second phase of 34 homes, including 10 affordable units dispersed across the site. The client was keen that the development should enhance the character of the town and create natural opportunities for people to congregate on, and move through, the previously closed site. Aware of the potentially contentious nature of development, the client consulted widely before a planning application was submitted to ensure local people's support for the project.

INTERPRETING SOUTHWOLD'S CHARACTER

Ash Sakula aimed to create a contemporary mixed-use community with a clear sense of identity. The design approach was led by first-hand experience of the texture and grain of the town: its ginnels (narrow alleyways cutting between buildings), gardens laden with plants, unexpected views, changes in scale and juxtaposition of materials (see Figure 2.4.1). Different shapes and sizes of building jostle together and there are often sudden changes in scale and colour; two-storey buildings nestle comfortably against four-storey buildings and no single material dominates (see Figure 2.4.2).

Ash Sakula spent time in the town to – as Robert Sakula describes – 'get under its skin'; observing its character, talking to local people and using this experience to inform the design process. This approach is applied to every part of the site, resulting in an evolving masterplan with a sense of particularity across the development. Each space, each corner and each edge has its

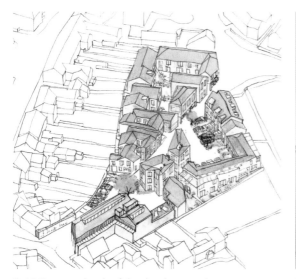

2.4.1 Concept sketch of the development in context

2.4.2 Building forms jostle together, evoking the character of the wider town

own character responding to adjacent buildings, views and light, creating a clear sense of identity.

The project focuses on Drayman Square, a new market square adjacent to the high street flanked by the low slung Adnams kitchen and wine store. This square is fronted by two tall buildings containing six apartments and a small shop with views towards St Edmund's Church.

From the square a residential street and a network of lanes and ginnels cut through the site toward Tibby's Green – the heart of the town – and connect into the wider context. To the west of the new street, houses form village-like clusters around gardens and yards informed by studies of the alleyways, yards and houses behind houses found across Southwold (*see* Figure 2.4.3). To the east, informal terraces culminate in a terrace of five three-storey homes offering views across Tibby's Green and defining the northern boundary of this green space (*see* Figure 2.4.4). The development has a distinctly urban character and density but this is softened by green edges of indigenous planting. While parking is provided for all new homes, on- and off-plot parking is designed into the network of yards and lanes without dominating the streetscape.

Drawing on the experience gained by spending time in the town, every house is different. Plan forms, floor heights and material details change, making each house unique, reminiscent of the irregular forms created by incremental growth visible elsewhere in Southwold (*see* Figure 2.4.5). There is a sense of gradual evolution and individual identity rather than a 'one size fits all' solution.

2.4.3 Intimate planted yards create clusters of homes

2.4.4 A three-storey terrace defines the north boundary of Tibby's Green

'We call it our modern cottage, it's bright, sunny, what else is there to say? It's great. It's what we were looking for … for about 10 years!'

Resident

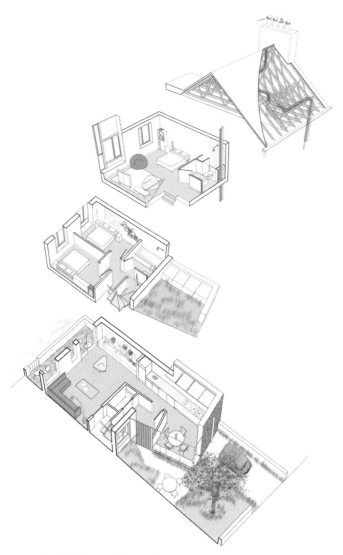

2.4.5 Sketch of a typical house layout

CHARACTER AND DETAIL

The form and materials respond to the scale and character of the wider town, while being distinctly contemporary. The barn-like form of the Adnams kitchen and wine store with glazed ends is clad in corrugated metal sheeting, whereas the lower rear café is extensively glazed and incorporates timber vats from the former brewery.

Buff brick predominates, sometimes left natural and in other places painted white or tarred black in the maritime tradition. Clay pantiles are used on pitched roofs throughout, while flat roofs are either sedum covered or are used as roof terraces for apartments. Bespoke timber-framed windows are placed differently in each

2.4.6 Windows protrude or recess from the building façades

2.4.7 The view to the church framed from the apartment building

home in response to light and views (*see* Figures 2.4.6 and 2.4.7). In some places these are recessed while in others they project forwards, creating a play of depth across the façades. Chimneys are not decorative but house flues from a mechanical ventilation and heat recovery system are located in each house.

References to the history of the town are cleverly integrated; decorative flint and brick garden walls continue the patchwork found across Southwold; brewery vats become seating snugs in the café, while timber piles from Southwold's beach groynes have been embedded in the surface of the square.

'Because of the high-quality materials that we used, the landscaping and the wonderful design, it should really stand the test of time and we will be proud of it for many years to come.'

James Hopkins, Hopkins Homes

CONCLUSION

The transformation of the former Adnams distribution depot creates desperately needed new homes and apartments in the heart of Southwold. The dense and intimate development is well connected into the pattern of streets, lanes and ginnels, extending the patchwork of the town and creating new routes through what was previously private land. By drawing inspiration from local scale, grain, materials and colour, the project successfully integrates with its historic context while developing a contemporary architectural language with a strong and distinctive character.

TRANSFORMATIONS

- **Character and sense of place**: careful studies of the site, its particularities and surroundings has led to a thoughtfully considered response to context with a clear sense of identity.

- **Integration**: the development knits into the fabric of the town, both adding to, and integrating with, the existing settlement. This makes the site permeable and welcoming to the community while making it easy for residents to take part in the life of the town.

- **Intimacy**: a dense development with a clear hierarchy of street, lane, alley and yard creates a sense of public and private space.

- **Avoiding pattern book homes**: an informal layout where each house is different creates a sense of individuality and incremental, organic growth, in keeping with the town's historic development.

- **Material and detail**: thorough attention to form, material and detail, the development has a sense of continuity with the wider town without resorting to pastiche. Buff brick, flint walls and painted surfaces reference the wider setting but are given a contemporary edge.

CREDITS

Client: Adnams / Hopkins Homes

Architect: Ash Sakula Architects

Contractor: Hopkins Homes

Structural engineer: Price & Myers

M+E engineer: Michael Popper Associates (now INGINE)

Cost consultant: Appleyards DWB

Awards: Housing Design Awards for Completed Scheme 2012; What House? Gold Award for Best Brownfield Development 2011; Housing Design Awards for Best Project 2008

2.5 THE AVENUE, SAFFRON WALDEN

Location: Saffron Walden, Essex, UK

Population: 15,504

Number of homes: 76 (25% affordable and 18 homes for the over 55s)

Contract value: £14m

Status: Completed 2014

Nestled around a magnificent avenue of mature lime trees at the edge of a conservation area, The Avenue creates clusters of new homes responding to the sensitive landscape and built form of a historic market town. The new homes range from one-bedroom flats to five-bedroom detached houses and include 18 flats and smaller cottages designed for the over-55 market organised in a series of character areas threading across the site and connecting into the town.

2.5.0 Aerial view of The Avenue in context

SITE AND CONTEXT

Saffron Walden is a characterful medieval market town located between London and Cambridge. Historically renowned for its wool trade and a strongly Puritan population during the seventeenth century, the town today finds itself in an area of considerable growth driven by an acceptance of longer-distance commutes to London and its proximity to Cambridge. Housing is in high demand, but much new development is located on the periphery of local towns and villages. Often remote from and poorly connected to local centres, these homes increase reliance on the car and do little to enhance community. In contrast, The Avenue provides new homes in the heart of Saffron Walden, set within an established mature landscape which includes over 150 existing trees, many with preservation orders.

The land belonged to the Quaker Friends' School (QFS), established on the site in 1879. QFS was intent on delivering a high-quality, financially viable project to fund school redevelopment while maintaining what was special about the mature landscape setting. The challenge for the architects was to create a feasible dense development while maintaining and enhancing the intrinsic qualities of the site.

Wide public consultation early in the design process and pre-planning engagement with the local authority aimed to generate support for the scheme from early in its gestation. The development was obliged to meet the requirements of the Essex Design Guide, the local authority design guidance first developed in 1973 on Townscape principles.[16] The guide interprets the form and character of towns and villages in Essex into a series of generic design tools to ensure new developments integrate with existing settlements. Despite best intentions, design guidance of this sort is often criticised for inadvertently leading to nondescript, 'anywhere' development. The design solution at The Avenue adopts these principles but creates a contemporary vernacular with a sense of individuality and informality through carefully considered material juxtapositions and formal relationships.

RESTORING THE AVENUE

The most notable features of the existing site were an avenue of lime trees extending north to south (see Figure 2.5.1) and a listed red brick water tower. An early design decision was to retain and restore this avenue and make it the heart of the scheme, which has since become a popular walking route into the town centre for local residents. Clusters of homes off this route respond to their immediate context; as many of the 150 mature trees as possible were retained through careful positioning and grouping of houses. A pedestrian and vehicle route, this is now a well-used public right of way connecting through the site to the town centre.

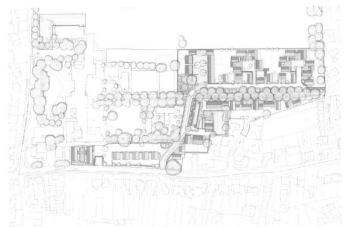

2.5.1 The existing tree-lined avenue at the heart of the site

2.5.2 Site plan

DEFINING CHARACTER AREAS

The design solution aimed to create a distinctive, integrated neighbourhood which reflected the pattern and character of the neighbouring townscape and landscape. The scheme takes cues from the grain and form of the town and site to create a series of 'character areas' tailored to their individual setting: Water Tower Place, The Entrance, The Avenue and The Courtyards (*see* Figure 2.5.2).

To the north of the site, Water Tower Place consists of a terrace of two-storey homes connected at ground floor by a flat-roofed utility area (*see* Figure 2.5.3). Appearing as a series of simple gable-ended forms, these reflect the form of the semi-detached homes opposite the site. The water tower is flanked by a terrace of red brick buildings responding to the material palette of the listed building and the town conservation area. Adjacent to the school, homes are intended for the over-55s market. A private formal garden is overlooked by cottages and an apartment building conceived as a large barn.

At the centre of the scheme is The Entrance, the main vehicular route into the site and characterised by terraces of houses with a parking court behind. To the south are The Avenue and The Courtyards. The Avenue is named for the mature lime trees flanking a new pedestrian and vehicle route through the site (*see* Figure 2.5.4). To the west, homes are detached and accessed directly from it. A brick boundary wall defines the eastern edge of The Avenue, punctured to access The Courtyards. Here, homes are tightly clustered around informal yards, giving a sense of intimacy to the scheme while maximising private space for each dwelling. These courtyards work hard as shared semi-public spaces. They have enough parking for up to 12 resident cars and four visitors

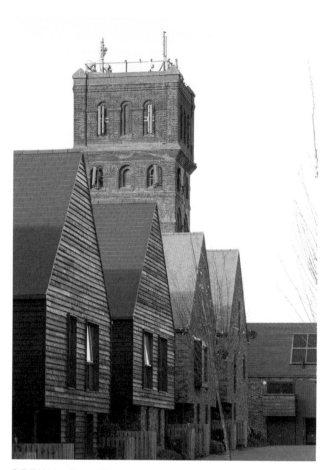

2.5.3 Water Tower Place

2.5.4 The Avenue

plus turning space, provide bin and bike stores for the cluster, have active frontages and allow access to up to five front doors, and create a sense of enclosure while maintaining 21-m distances between dwellings to limit overlooking (see Figure 2.5.5). Homes

2.5.5 The Courtyards are hardworking shared spaces with a strong sense of enclosure which maintaining a 21m distance between dwellings

2.5.6 Simple forms and detailing with irregular window arrangements create a distinctly contemporary language

have a mix of single and double garages. These barn-like elements are pushed back from the houses, adding a sense of informality to the overall composition of each courtyard. From the shared courtyard, each house has direct access to sizable private gardens with views across the school grounds.

CREATING VARIETY AND INDIVIDUALITY

At The Avenue, each home has been designed in response to its unique location, landscape, aspect and prospect. House types use a 'kit of parts' to create individuality and variety while maintaining economies of repetition. Building forms and house typologies draw from vernacular traditions, reflecting local agricultural buildings and the town houses found in the local neighbourhood. Forms are simple, extruded and generally pitch-roofed. Materials draw from the local context; a mix of traditional materials such as red brick, black weatherboards, render and timber shingles expresses individual plots within each courtyard cluster. Variety and distinctiveness is extended through use of dormer, projecting bay and corner windows, recessed front doors and simple cantilevered porch canopies which add identity to individual dwellings. Detailing is stripped back but distinctly contemporary, with minimal eaves and verges (see Figure 2.5.6).

'It is a pretty unique design style, but still picking up on certain parts of the local design vernacular. When we look out the front of the house, although we're looking out onto a roadway, there isn't any concrete, there isn't any tarmac. There's a nice contrast of brick to woods to greenery. That attention to detail means that you've got the variety that everybody seeks in the places that they want to live, rather than just living in another box next to another box.'

Callum, resident

CONCLUSION

Clusters of new homes respond to local building traditions and nestle into a mature landscape. By grouping new homes around the avenue of mature lime trees, a strong focus is made of the landscape setting and a historic public right of way is reinstated as a linking thread through the development. With a mix of tenures and 25% affordable housing alongside housing for the over 55s, the project addresses the local challenges of a lack of affordable homes and the ability to downsize in place for local people as well as creating a socially diverse extension to the community.

TRANSFORMATIONS

- **Mixed-use neighbourhoods**: the scheme provides a financially viable mixed-use neighbourhood. It balances demand for commuter homes with concerns about affordable homes for people working locally while allowing long-term residents to downsize in place.

- **Challenging pattern book homes**: the use of a 'kit of parts' to generate distinctive house types challenges the use of 'identikit' pattern book homes and demonstrates how a more contextual approach can be achieved.

- **Early engagement**: early consultation with local residents and the planning authority helped secure local buy-in and resulted in a sympathetic but contemporary addition to a conservative market town.

- **Integration**: connecting The Avenue to the local surroundings through pedestrian ways helps to integrate the development into the local context.

- **Character and sense of place**: the use of character areas creates a sense of distinctiveness within a sizable development. These areas have different densities, typologies, types of space and material finishes, creating individuality within a larger whole and responding to their immediate context.

- **Courtyards**: the careful design of hard-working courtyards accommodates parking and services within a compact semi-public space. This urban-feeling space creates clusters of neighbours while allowing residents to retreat into their homes and gardens.

- **Simple forms and materials**: simple prismatic forms respond to the vernacular but are stripped of detail, lending a contemporary aesthetic. A limited palette of materials creates individuality while maintaining a coherence to the overall development.

CREDITS

Client: Hill

Architect: Pollard Thomas Edwards

Contractor/Developer: Hill

Local Authority: Uttlesford District Council

Structural engineer: Rossi Long

M&E engineer: M Rogerson Ltd

Landscape: Elwood Landscape Design

Awards: RIBA National Award 2016; RIBA Regional Award 2016; Housing Design Award 2015; What House? Gold Award 2014; Housing Design Project Award 2011

Location: Gistel, Flanders, Belgium

Population: 12,063

Number of homes: 13 apartments

Contract value: €1.57m

Status: Completed 2015

Flanders' towns are facing challenges in common with many small settlements in north-west Europe, with increasing numbers of households, an ageing population, sprawling urban areas and diminishing affordability. Located on a backland site in the centre of Gistel in West Flanders, this project illustrates the potential of integrating new mixed tenure housing in the centre of a small town. Through creative urban design 13 new homes are woven into the heart of the settlement, creating a new public space, a rejuvenated community hub and reinforcing the fabric of the town centre.

2.6.0 The project in its street context

SITE AND CONTEXT

Gistel is a municipality in West Flanders comprising the towns of Gistel, Moere, Snaaskere and Zevokote. It is a town of medieval origin characterised by long, narrow plots perpendicular to both the main coastal road and a lane leading to Ten Putte Abbey, set in the marshy hinterland. Between these two streets lies a deep urban block with a low-slung pantile-roofed inn at its north-eastern corner (see Figure 2.6.1). The project site frames the inn on two sides, fronting the abbey lane and a perpendicular lane and backing onto neighbouring gardens to the rear.

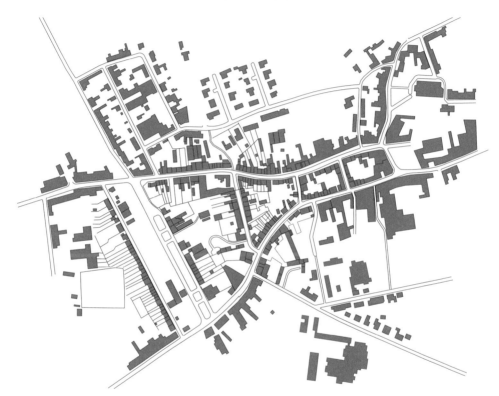

2.6.1 Site plan

A collaboration between a housing association, the town council and the ministry of public works, the project creates 13 new apartments, a new social space and a new public space. Initially planned as housing for the elderly, the final project mixes elderly residents in ground floor Lifetime Homes apartments and social tenants on the first floor (see Figures 2.6.2 and 2.6.3). The project was complex for its size and had a long gestation. Initially held back by planning processes, land purchase and grant negotiations, it reached site in 2011. However, bankruptcy of the contractor for the public square and delays in utility connections caused the project to take a further four years on site before final completion in 2015.

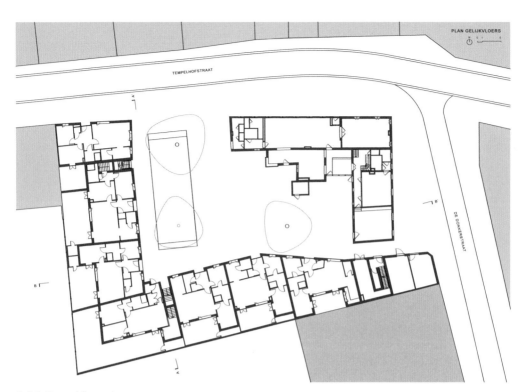

2.6.2 Ground floor plan

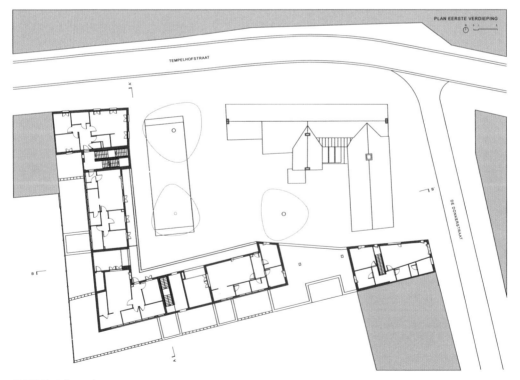

2.6.3 First floor plan

CREATING AN OUTDOOR ROOM

Rather than simply completing the gaps in the street, the design brings a public route through the site and creates a new courtyard at the centre of the town (see Figure 2.6.4). The housing is pushed to the rear of the site, providing space around the historic inn and creating a central courtyard. Crafted in a simple palette of red brick pavers, a square of grass and young trees, this new brick outdoor room connects out onto the surrounding streets. This is a public space for the life of the town, a sunny café terrace for the inn and a softer garden by the wrap of housing.

The organisation and scale of the housing shares similarities with the traditional almshouse model, based around a shared focal space, and hints at how this model may be reinterpreted for the twenty-first century.[17] The scale of the apartment block follows the ridge height of the inn and the surrounding context, its scale sensitively knitting into the existing town (see Figure 2.6.5). Alongside the inn, the apartment block narrows and a public passageway feeds in, connecting to the street and increasing the permeability of the site.

2.6.4 The courtyard between the inn and new housing is the heart of the project

2.6.5 The massing of the project adjusts to the context

INTIMACY AND COMMUNITY

The ambition to create a communal courtyard results in a long and relatively shallow apartment block with compact planning and small patio gardens. Ground floor apartments are accessed from individual front doors facing the courtyard, while first floor apartments are reached by a shared stair and open access deck. Where the block meets the coast road it rises to three storeys with a more formal frontage, announcing its presence on the main street (see Figure 2.6.6).

These distortions, and the difficult corner conditions, result in 13 unique two-bed apartment types ranging from 76 m² to 81 m².

2.6.6 The form of the housing responds to the surrounding building forms

In contrast to the narrow historic plots lining the street, the thin perimeter block necessitates wide aspect apartments with a broad proportion which repeats across the block. This is emphasised by the timber-lined first floor deck, set back from the façade and overhanging roof. At ground floor, L-shaped apartments are accessed from the courtyard and face outwards to more private patio gardens at the rear. All are designed to Lifetime Homes standards with minimal circulation and a substantial living and dining room at its centre, from which the main bedroom and bathroom is accessed. At first floor, long, shallow apartments are accessed from two generous staircases opening onto a deck overlooking the courtyard. A planned lift was omitted, meaning the first floor apartments are rented to younger residents. The access deck continues across the full width of the apartments. Living rooms open out to this 'terrace', an extension of the apartment sheltered by a deep eaves, overlooking the garden below, the low inn roof and beyond to the church tower (see Figure 2.6.7).

The materials are restrained but contextual, necessitated by the desire to use the available budget to maximise daylight and external spaces. A grey lime-washed budget brick is used throughout, a common local material treatment. An irregular arrangement of grey timber-framed windows change in size and proportion depending on their aspect. Windows are hardwood and doors are recessed. A change in material from brick to timber suggests a threshold to interior space, a deep threshold between public and private space that offers the opportunity for socialising with those outside. Emerging onto the timber-lined first floor access terrace, large opening windows encourage residents to inhabit these shared spaces, while living rooms open onto red brick-lined terraces, contrasting warm brickwork walls and floors with timber cladding.

Internally, laminated timber beams are exposed and express a regular rhythm within the apartments. At first floor, these beams follow the gentle pitch of the roof and create a feeling of openness and generosity to the spaces (see Figure 2.6.8). Elsewhere, detailing is economical and direct. The sense is of an overall wholeness – one that is contemporary in form and detail but which resonates with the scale and grain of its surrounding context. Throughout the project views of the town are framed through large windows or off the access deck, connecting residents to the wider community.

2.6.7 A continuous access deck offers views across the town

2.6.8 Internally, a simple material palette continues. Timber beams are exposed and large windows allow in a generous amount of light.

CONCLUSION

Carefully considered urban design has changed a derelict backland site into a new piece of the town, integrating housing, a public space and a social hub. The ambition to create communal space at the heart of the town required careful consideration of the building form and massing to respond to the historic seventeenth-century inn and the character of the two streets, while creating distinctive places in which to live. The resulting outdoor room is a focus around which the everyday social life of the town can unfold.

TRANSFORMATIONS

- **Urban design**: the project breaks the pattern of the street and introduces a new opportunity for social interaction in the form of a small square for residents and a terrace for the historic inn.

- **New uses**: the project introduces compact homes for later living and social rent into the heart of the town on a derelict site, rejuvenating a historic inn back into a social space for the town.

- **Grain**: the scale and form of the project is carefully woven into its context, its form rising and falling in response to the character of each street and proximity to the historic inn.

- **Economic use of material**: the material palette responds to the historic inn and dominance of brick in the surroundings and uses timber linings to announce entrances and thresholds.

- **Framing**: key views of the town are framed by large windows, connecting residents to their surroundings.

CREDITS

Client: WoonWel Housing Association

Architect: Witherford Watson Mann Architects

Architectural support: Bureau Bouwtechniek

Structural engineer: BAS / Dirk Jaspaert

M&E engineer: Studiebureau Paul Vandenberghe

Contractor: Simoens

Landscape architect (design of public square): Paul Deroose

2.7 STEEPLETON RETIREMENT COMMUNITY

> **Location:** Tetbury, Gloucestershire, UK
>
> **Population:** 5,472
>
> **Number** of homes: 113 later living apartments (68 completed)
>
> **Contract** value: £23m
>
> **Status:** Phase 1 completed 2019

The average age of the inhabitants of towns and villages is increasing at a higher rate than the rest of the country[18] but opportunities for people to age in place are often limited and many elderly people face increasing isolation. Steepleton demonstrates how homes for later living can draw on local character to successfully integrate into the fabric of a historic town in an area of Outstanding Natural Beauty (a designated exceptional landscape), counteracting isolation through social interaction and the provision of high-quality social space.

2.7.0 Steepleton seen from the street. A stone boundary wall, gabled form and expressed chimneys draw from the character of the town.

SITE AND CONTEXT

Tetbury is a picturesque market town located in the Cotswolds. The town boasts over 1,300 years recorded history; however the wealth of the town emerged during the late Middle Ages. Renowned for its wool and yarn, the town core displays the trappings of success with many fine stone houses which belonged to wool merchants. It reached the height of its prosperity in the sixteenth and seventeenth centuries and the thriving town boasts a wealth of heritage from this period, including the iconic market house, built in 1655. By the early nineteenth century the wool trade had declined and the town was largely bypassed by the Industrial Revolution. However, with the arrival of the railway in 1889, the town expanded and is today twice the size it was in the eighteenth century, sustained by tourism and light manufacturing industry located around the edges of the town.

The 0.8 ha site was formerly home to an industrial production facility. Relocation of the business gave the opportunity to redevelop the site as a residential neighbourhood and an extension of the low-density residential areas to the north, west and south of the site. These areas consist of a variety of detached two-storey cottages and larger houses built between the Victorian era and today.

Developer PegasusLife has developed a reputation for design-led retirement homes aimed at the premium end of the market. The design brief asked for an environment that would enable supported independence and develop a sense of community between residents and with the wider town. Shared spaces inside and out needed to be designed to encourage social interaction. The homes themselves are a mix of one- and two-bed apartments, all designed to comply with Lifetime Homes standards and designed using the principles of the HAPPI (Housing our Ageing Population: Panel for Innovation) report.

COURTYARD CLUSTERS

Drawing inspiration from Gloucestershire farmsteads and research into almshouses, two-storey buildings cluster at a domestic scale around open courtyards with one side open to the site boundaries (see Figures 2.7.1 and 2.7.2). These clusters aim to provide a sense of identity, security and belonging between small groups of residents within the wider site and give the development a village character with a familiar, tightknit urban grain.

A line of mature trees is maintained along the public street edge. An undulating stone wall creates a perimeter, dropping in height to allow views into the landscaped courtyards. A pair of dual gables perpendicular to the road front the street, a motif found elsewhere in the town and one which, while holding the neighbouring

2.7.1 Site plan in context

2.7.2 A 3D model shows the scale of clusters in relation to the surroundings

building lines, gives the project a sense of public presence. Views between the gables focus on a small, publicly accessible café and a central landscaped courtyard with a swimming pond flanked by the shared facilities.

Townscape markers – a lychgate, a projecting stone chimney gable marking the eastern entrance and a dovecote stair which ends the long view from the site entrance – create recognisable features to aid navigation throughout the site (see Figure 2.7.3).

From one main vehicle entry a circular roadway connects a series of hard landscaped yards, designed as shared surfaces with brick paving. Parking is integrated into the courtyards and in undercroft parking for reduced accessibility homes; tucked away, this does not overbear on the shared streetscapes which feel welcoming to pedestrians.

2.7.3 A giant sundial marks the social heart of the village

Material choices reference the Cotswold vernacular and respond to the Cotswold Design Code. At ground level, Cotswold stone gives texture and relief to the base of the buildings and boundary walls, unifying the courtyard clusters and creating a sense of permanence and protection. Above, a lime wash coloured render is complemented by contemporary dormers and grey hoods to balconies, articulating and breaking up longer façades while creating a coherent but varied architectural language.

ENCOURAGING SOCIAL INTERACTION

The development contains 113 later living apartments, typically one-bedroom apartments at ground floor level with larger two-bedroom maisonettes above. Around each courtyard at the heart of the cluster is the 'ambulatory', a cloister-like walkway wrapping around both ground and first floor levels. This acts as a protected circulation space but also a social space. It breaks up and animates the courtyard elevations and controls views across the courtyards. Vertical Douglas fir adds warmth and creates a more intimate scale to these spaces. Interaction is gently encouraged; at points, timber portals set into the balustrade create places to look out across the courtyards or greet neighbours, while seating is clustered outside the entrances to apartments, encouraging neighbourliness (see Figure 2.7.4).

2.7.4 Timber frames create moments for interaction within the courtyards

2.7.5 Courtyards have their own character, such as this one with a gardening courtyard and a walled garden

Around and within the courts are landscaped gardens and allotments. Each apartment has its own outdoor space, individual kitchen gardens at ground floor and balconies above. Each courtyard across the development has different uses – growing, gardening and walking through (*see* Figure 2.7.5).

At the heart of the development is a 'village hall', a barn-like structure with a sundial tower containing communal facilities such as a dining room, residents' lounge, IT facilities, care and therapy rooms and an exercise room. Here is the social heart of the scheme, where spaces for eating, exercise and relaxing encourage interaction between residents around an outdoor swimming pond (see Figure 2.7.6).

2.7.6 The residents' lounge and spa overlook the swimming pond

CONCLUSION

Steepleton has created a new community for later living on a previous industrial site near the centre of Tetbury. Careful detailing connects to the vernacular tradition of the Cotswold setting while developing a contemporary architectural language of dormers, bay windows and ambulatories. Breaking down a large development of 113 apartments into smaller clusters informed by almshouses and farmsteads gently encourages a sense of neighbourliness. Consciously designing for social interaction from the scale of the context to the urban design of the site to the courtyard cluster and the home itself creates a sense of belonging and can counter social isolation, a particularly important consideration for the rapidly ageing populations of smaller settlements.

TRANSFORMATIONS

- **Courtyard clusters**: drawing from agricultural forms and almshouses, to create domestic scale courtyards with different characters that encourage sociability and a sense of community.

- **Community infrastructure**: the wider community is welcomed into the site, particularly through a publicly accessible café and library/study, knitting the project into its wider community.

- **Material and detail**: a family of architectural details drawn from the context – dry and mortared stone walls, dormers, chimneys, double gables and a consistent series of window shapes and sizes – give a consistency and variety to the project.

- **Townscape markers**: a sequence of architectural 'moments' creates a memorable streetscape through the development that evokes the feeling of the medieval town.

CREDITS

Client: PegasusLife

Architects: Proctor and Matthews Architects

Main contractor: Speller Metcalf

Planning consultant: Barton Willmore

Structural and civil engineers and transport consultants: Peter Brett Associates LLP

M&E consultant: Max Fordham

Landscape architects: Camlins

Geotechnical engineer: WYG Management Services – Engineering

Archaeologist: CgMs Consulting (London)

Project manager: Tweeds Construction Consultancy (London)

Ecologist: Ecoschemes

Public relations: Green Issues Communique

Social policy and care advisor: Contacting Consulting

Arboriculturalist: Tree Maintenance Limited

Awards: Housing Design Awards, HAPPI Award, 2019; RIBA South West Award 2019; Shortlisted, RIBA McEwan Award 2019; Housing Design Awards, Project Winner, 2015

CHAPTER 3

Town Centres: Building the Heart of a Community

3.1 THE CHANGING NATURE OF THE TOWN CENTRE

Historically, town centres were the focus of life for their communities. A locus for trade, exchange, social interaction and celebration, town centres were at the heart of civic life. During the twentieth century town centres developed a reliance on retail as a focus for their activity, and new infrastructure – such as roads dividing or bypassing centres, out-of-town retail developments, under-used heritage assets and uninviting public realm – have led to the decline of many town centres.[1] The impact of the 2008 financial crisis and the continuing rise of online shopping, now accounting for 20% of all UK retail sales, have caused rising vacancy rates, with one in 12 shops having closed over the past five years.[2] Services such as banks, post offices, medical centres and schools have suffered drastic cuts and closures, with many centralised or moved out of town. Combined with a decline in investment and reducing footfall, the outlook for town centres seems increasingly bleak. The 2011 predication by Mary Portas that the high street could disappear may yet prove accurate.[3]

There is a pressing need to rethink what our town centres are for and how they can be reimagined. With increasing political interest in smaller communities, architects and designers are well-placed to lead the way in considering the future of town centres. This chapter explores a series of projects where the fortunes of town centres have been radically altered, diversifying the focus beyond retail to explore futures founded on local identity, a sense of community and new civic functions.

THE DECLINE OF RETAIL AND COMMUNITY SERVICES

The fortunes of town centres and high streets have fluctuated over time and vary dramatically across the country, although the current decline is widespread. Studies by the New Economics Foundation (NEF) since 2002 have identified a growing number of 'ghost towns' suffering from the rapid disappearance of independent shops and businesses and an increasing domination by global and national chain stores.[4] Between 1995 and 2000 one-fifth of banks, post offices, corner shops and independent retailers in the UK ceased trading. This decline has continued; 1,772 stores closed in 2017, an increase on the previous year.[5] This is driven by a 'perfect storm' of the increase in out-of-town retail, the impact of online shopping and convenience culture, the ongoing repercussions of the 2008 economic crash and austerity politics, and decreasing consumer confidence and footfall.[6] The impact of this loss of easy access to local shops and services includes increased reliance on fast food, and losses of financial literacy, community based part-time employment, social capital and diversity in the retail environment.[7]

Alongside the decline of high street retail centres, town centres have suffered the loss of many service centre functions such as post offices, banks and public services. The number of Post Office branches has halved since the 1980s[8] and one-third of all bank branches closed between 2015 and 2019.[9] The ongoing impact of austerity and the reduction in funding for public services and institutions since 2008 has led to increasing consolidation of local authority assets in major service centres. This has also been instrumental in the shift of schools and medical centres to the peripheries of towns, away from their cores. This reduces footfall to centres, increases car use and can result in a loss of community cohesion. One response can be seen in the growth of community asset transfer, whereby the management of assets such as libraries and town halls are transferred to community organisations to maintain or enhance the social, environmental or economic benefit of these assets to their communities.

THE HIGH STREET BEYOND RETAIL

There have been a variety of responses to the crisis facing town centres. The well-publicised *Portas Review* of 2011 offered a stark assessment of the challenges but emphasised the importance of the high street and town centre as the heart of British Society.[10] Twenty-seven 'Portas Pilots' were established to test retail-led measures to improve high streets. However, as the recent second *Grimsey Review* suggests, retail can no longer be the anchor it once was for town centres. These centres need to be re-thought as community hubs with a wider appeal.[11] The UK government's expert panel for high streets suggests that to survive town centres need to attract people for a wide range of activities, such as dining, culture and the arts, sport and leisure, medical services, living and entertainment.[12] The Scottish *National Review of Town Centres*[13] and the National Assembly for Wales' *Regeneration of Town Centres Report*[14] both identified that revitalisation should look more broadly at a diverse mix of uses, including parks, leisure, culture, learning, working and homes as well as retail. Increasingly, people are looking for 'experiences'; while retail remains important, activities that serve the community, entertainment and pop-up events are becoming an increasingly important aspect of the individual and collective experience people are searching for in choosing where to live, work and play.[15]

A RENEWED COMMITMENT

The UK government has recently strengthened its commitment to town centres. The £675m Future High Street Fund aims to explore new approaches to high streets, acknowledging that the way people use their towns has changed. The funding is focused on improving transport, vehicle and pedestrian flow, housing and office space and tackling persistent vacancy.[16] The Scotland Town Centre Fund has committed £50m in 2019–20 for place-based investments to encourage diversification of town centres. The fund aims to contribute to transformative investments to enable places to thrive through themes such as increasing town centre living, enabling enterprise, accessible public services, digital technology and planning innovation.[17] Regionally, the West Midlands Combined Authority is injecting almost £20m into local authority plans to regenerate five town centres. Recent initiatives – such as the RIBA's Future Town competition – demonstrate the desire from practice to explore these issues, but we need to do more. There is a significant opportunity for the profession to engage with these programmes and lead the way in radically rethinking how we revitalise town centres, re-establishing their diversity and social role, encouraging local ownership and sifting their emphasis from places to buy to places to be.[18]

RETHINKING TOWN CENTRES

The challenge for designers is how to shift the emphasis from the high street as a place of retail to rediscovering its role in the rhythms and rituals of the everyday life. Rethinking the future of town centres requires understanding of the local community, its dynamic and its practices. Knowledge of the changing patterns of work, leisure and travel of residents and visitors can help designers understand places through the eyes of the people who use them.[19] Ideas need to work with the existing built fabric and often this will mean considering the purpose of buildings and spaces and their adaptation to maintain relevance. Vacant buildings are common, often left behind as retail and families move out to town peripheries. English Heritage and the Architectural Heritage Fund have been instrumental in bringing historic buildings back into use, but there are complexities in adapting existing buildings and ingenuity is needed in their adaptation and transformation. They offer opportunities to introduce new short- or long-term uses or create community uses fostering social interaction. Town centres need to be attractive to residents and visitors, diverse and enjoyable places to be. They should be thought of as multi-functional spaces; not just a place to shop but also places to live, for work and for leisure. New housing in town centres, either above shops, in new mixed-use developments or in converted buildings is vital in reversing their decline. Questions such as how space is used, by whom, who owns it and who benefits from change are vitally important in creating thriving town centres for all.

The profession is well placed to respond to these questions. Our skills in acting as mediators in complex design processes can help bring together local stakeholders and the wider community to redefine town centres, bringing together a wide range of uses and activities – green space, housing, activities and events, leisure, arts and culture, health, education and public services alongside retail – to create vibrant, multi-layered places rich in social interaction.

3.2 WARWICK COMMUNITY HALL, BURFORD

> **Location:** Burford, Oxfordshire, UK
>
> **Population:** 1,422
>
> **Contract** value: £3.2m
>
> **Status:** Completed 2017

A new community complex reimagines a dilapidated parish hall adjacent to a Grade I listed church creating a new social heart for community and church alike. Careful craftsmanship and a sense of continuity with the wider town embed the new hall into its sensitive historic context.

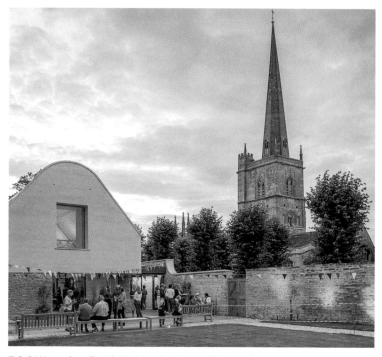

3.2.0 Warwick Hall with St John the Baptist Church beyond

SITE AND CONTEXT

Burford is a picturesque Cotswold town located between Oxford and Cheltenham. A prosperous hub for the wool trade during the medieval period, the town was bypassed by the railway and suffered economic decline. More recently, its unspoilt heritage has attracted day-trippers and tourism, changing the town's fortunes.

An important site on the town tour is the magnificent Grade I listed St John the Baptist Church, one of the largest of the Cotswold wool churches. Begun in the eleventh century, finished in the fifteenth century and modified in the Victorian period, the church is one of the top 10 most visited churches in the country. The adjacent Warwick Hall, a converted fifteenth-century residence, had been used as a church school before accommodating a variety of church and community groups. A historically complex building, it contained elements of a variety of building typologies and had been variously extended and remodelled. However, with poor access and catering facilities it no longer met contemporary requirements; the facilities had become completely inadequate for both the congregation of the church and the wider community.

The brief set out to bring together the church and community by creating a new flexible and inclusive facility that would become the heart of civic life. Burford has historically lacked a town hall, so the aim was to provide a new adaptable space usable for a range of activities such as dance classes, a crèche, a day centre for the elderly, performances, lectures and even church services. Alongside this hall, the brief asked for a community café, meeting rooms, toilets and a large basement store, all situated within the garden of the original Warwick Hall.

As church architect for St John the Baptist in Burford, Acanthus Clews was appointed to explore the potential of the Warwick Hall site in anticipation of the freehold returning to the church in 2012. The aim was to restore the significance of Warwick Hall by removing poor-quality additions and creating a new complex that respected its sensitive historic context. The site bounds the fifteenth century churchyard and shares a boundary with the Grade II* listed Great Almshouses. Next to the River Windrush mill race, the site is considered the heart of the Saxon settlement and benefits from views across the churchyard to open countryside.

The project attracted considerable scrutiny from Historic England and the Oxfordshire Diocesan Advisory Committee. Detailed archaeological and architectural assessment of the buildings and site was required to determine which elements were detrimental to the existing listed building and would be suitable for removal. To ensure the building design met the needs of the local community, numerous exhibitions and workshops were held during the project development to ensure a positive contribution from the community to the design process. One outcome to emerge was the potential to strengthen the partnership between the town council and Burford Charity Trustees to deliver key services, such as elderly day care.

DEFINING OLD AND NEW

Any new addition needed to respect the sensitive nature of the context and maintain a domestic scale so as not to overpower the church, existing hall and almshouses. In order to create a series of spaces which respect the delicate historic setting, the larger elements of the new building were broken up and separated by a cluster of smaller support structures, reducing their impact. The new form reinforces the boundary of the town and acts as a bookend to the settlement. Each hall is expressed as an individual pitched roof volume set back from the churchyard wall and gable of the existing Warwick Hall, creating a clear hierarchy of old and new. The gable of a smaller volume containing a meeting room echoes the form of the Warwick Hall facing the churchyard (*see* Figure 3.2.1). The rounded gable of a larger volume containing the new hall is oriented along the boundary wall towards the mill race.

3.2.1 The old and new gables facing the churchyard

Access to the new building was relocated to the churchyard side of the site, reorienting the building and creating a new relationship with the church. Punching through the existing stone wall, this enables level access to the new building via a new entrance and foyer. This creates a central heart, the focus of the life of the building and a meeting space between the refurbished and new halls (*see* Figures 3.2.2 and 3.2.3). Importantly, it allows the two main halls to be booked and used independently. The existing hall is returned to its original proportions and carefully conserved.

The choice of materials was particularly important in this historic context, and materials and techniques have been chosen to match the church and townscape character. Stonework grounds the building in its context and site. A seamless repair using stone reclaimed from site demolition raises the boundary wall level alongside the churchyard, allowing the new building to tuck in behind this strong edge. This rough stonework contrasts with new

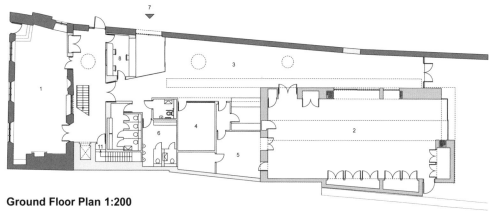

Ground Floor Plan 1:200

1.	Existing Warwick Hall	7.	Main entrance
2.	New Hall	8.	Staff office
3.	Cafe reception area	9.	External terrace
4.	Meeting room	10.	Plant
5.	Kitchen	11.	To basement store
6.	Toilets		

3.2.2 Ground floor plan

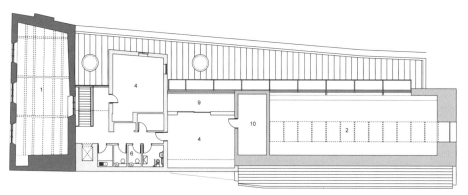

First Floor Plan 1:200

1.	Existing Warwick Hall	7.	Main entrance
2.	New Hall	8.	Staff office
3.	Cafe reception area	9.	External terrace
4.	Meeting room	10.	Plant
5.	Kitchen	11.	To basement store
6.	Toilets		

3.2.3 First floor plan

sanded stone ashlar gables (*see* Figure 3.2.4). These are carefully crafted; each course was meticulously drawn out and aligned with the openings. Natural slate roofs and local limestone embed the project in the town and allow other more contemporary materials, such as zinc and structural glazing, to be incorporated comfortably.

3.2.4 The connection between old and new

Inside, two stone walls are left exposed, one running the length of the church wall and a second framing the stair, giving a sense of weight to the space and aiding navigation. A lightweight circulation spine connects the boundary wall to the halls and frames views towards the church tower. The new spaces are finished in robust, simple materials. Clean lines, generous rooflight and framed views contrast with the historic detail of Warwick Hall and the character of the exposed wall.

FLEXIBILITY AND ADAPTABILITY

The new hall needed to cater for a wide range of activities and as such has to be incredibly flexible – able to be a private or 'black box' space but equally a completely open hall full of light and views. Its height needed to be minimised to reduce its impact on the sensitive churchyard and neighbouring buildings. An asymmetric roof profile was developed with full-length clerestory glazing facing the churchyard and a central rooflight which minimises the ridge height and externally conceals the rooflight from view (*see* Figures 3.2.5 and 3.2.6). Sliding screens, glass sliding doors and blackout blinds give flexibility to quickly transform the space.

Cross Section 1:50

1. New Hall
2. Cafe reception area
3. Basement store
4. Churchyard
5. Almshouses

3.2.5 Cross-section through the new hall

3.2.6 View from the new hall to the café beyond

CONCLUSION

The new Warwick Hall has created a series of public facilities through a bold redevelopment project that aims to unite the church and community. The challenging nature of the historically sensitive site has driven a design response that reorients the hall towards the church and clusters new facilities behind an enclosing wall. The success of the project is best measured in the community's use of the centre. Alongside a popular café, it hosts a wide range of regular and one-off activities, including community and business meetings, mother and baby groups, exercise and dance classes, the Women's Institute, health and well-being meet ups, music performances, art exhibitions and the annual Burford Festival, demonstrating its key place in the rhythm of the town's life.

TRANSFORMATIONS

- **A heart for the community**: the project creates new community spaces and facilities catering for a wide range of activities located in the heart of the town.

- **Form and volume**: the careful composition and grain of the volumes breaks up the scale of the building, expressing deference to its listed surroundings and embedding it in its place.

- **Orientation**: reorienting access to the building establishes a strong relationship with the church while creating level access and allowing the existing hall to be returned to its original form.

- **Crafted materials**: the careful choice of locally specific materials creates a sense of continuity while contemporary detailing of the new addition clearly expresses the difference between old and new.

CREDITS

Client: St John the Baptist Church, Burford

Architects: Acanthus Clews Architects

Main contractors: Edgar Taylor Ltd

Quantity surveyors: BAQUS

Structural engineers: Price & Myers

M&E engineers: Environmental Engineering Partnership

Landscape architects: Clews Landscape Architects

Audio visual consultants: Smart Sense

Lighting designers: Firefly Lighting Design

Acoustic engineers: Arup Acoustic

Awards: RIBA National Award Winner; RIBA South Award Winner; RIBA South Conservation Award Winner; EASA National Churches Trust, President's Award; Civic Voice Design Award Winner; Civic Voice Contribution to Conservation Areas Award Winner; Civic Trust National Design Award, Winner; RICS South East Community Benefit Award, Highly Commended; Architects' Journal Retrofit of the Year Award Winner; Architects' Journal Architecture Awards, Heritage Project of the Year 2017; Architects' Journal Architecture Awards, Design of the Year 2017

Location: Northallerton, North Yorkshire, UK

Population: 16,832

Contract value: £975,000

Status: Completed 2017

Recent decades have seen a multitude of new out-of-town retail units built on the peripheries of small settlements, drawing shoppers and the life out of town centres. This project demonstrates an alternative vision by sensitively integrating a 900 m² retail store on a brownfield site in the centre of a North Yorkshire town. Embedding the new store within the community prevented loss of a major retailer to a peripheral location, strengthened the retail offer and revived a neglected corner of the historic town centre.

3.3.0 Stepping gables break up the form of the building

SITE AND CONTEXT

Northallerton is a thriving historic market town set between the Yorkshire Dales and the North Yorkshire Moors. Dating back to the Roman period, the town has long been a transport hub due to its position on the Great North Road between London and Edinburgh. An important religious centre during the medieval period, trade and industry grew in importance, strengthened by the arrival of the railway in the nineteenth century. The historic heart of the town has a strong urban grain of long plots with a narrow street frontage either side of a tapering high street. Beyond the historic centre, the town was greatly expanded in the late twentieth century by low density suburban development which surrounds the dense urban core.

Located at the northern end of Northallerton High Street, the former Rutson Hospital occupied a number of historic listed buildings which over time were extended with poor-quality additions. Relocating to new purpose-built premises, the site was in occasional use by NHS workers as a car park but its ramshackle buildings and high perimeter wall contributed little to the character of the town or its economy.

The project, developed by Jomast Developments, aimed to introduce a mixed-use scheme to redevelop this brownfield site and integrate it back into the town centre. Consisting of a new 900 m² food store, a bar/restaurant and car parking, the project aimed to rejuvenate and extend the high street, strengthening the town's retail core. With Marks & Spencer considering moving out of the town due to the constraints of their small existing store, securing this key tenant kept the store in the town and bucked the trend of large retailers moving to the outskirts of towns. Maintaining the presence of a high-end tenant can support other high street shops and boost local employment.

INTEGRATING A LARGE BUILDING INTO THE HISTORIC CONTEXT

The design of the new building aimed to integrate a new sizable retail space into a sensitive historic fabric. The site presented a number of challenges to the designers. Located within a conservation area and next to Grade II listed buildings and in close proximity to the market hall, the design had to respect the scale and character of the surrounding urban grain. A roundabout to the east created a curved boundary and limited options for the location of car park access. A particular challenge was creating a usable car park which was adequate to support the expected number of shoppers.

In response, the store is located to the south of the site, fronting Friarage Street, with a small car park contained between the store and the burgage plots to the north. The design draws from the strong pattern of long, thin burgage plots with strong street frontages found throughout the historic town. The overall footprint of the new store is divided into a series of parallel pitched roof volumes that respond in scale to their surroundings. To the east the building steps to follow the curving street edge, while to the west a more subtle stepping follows the line of the neighbouring historic plots (see Figure 3.3.1). The building mass steps down as it approaches the street. A lower entrance pavilion and a small public space which take up changes in level are accessed from Friarage Street. Subtle changes in height and form give the building a sense of irregularity and breaks down the mass of a large building footprint to a scale that sits comfortably in its setting.

3.3.1 The stepping building form facing the street

DESIGNING THE RETAIL ENVIRONMENT

The design uses passive design principles to reduce energy demand from lighting. With the increasing emphasis on designing sustainable buildings in light of the recent declarations of climate emergency and movements such as Architects Declare, in-depth consideration of how buildings are lit, heated, cooled and ventilated is of increasing importance. Maximising daylight through expanses of curtain walling, the building is carefully designed to take advantage of low-angle sun to pre-heat key spaces and reduce artificial lighting. A plant area at high level is concealed by perforated brickwork and a large, concealed roof opening. Marks & Spencer was involved in the design process to ensure the proposed building suited its needs and fitted with its sustainability agenda, Plan A. Internally, the scheme has been designed to be loose fit and flexible to accommodate different uses and tenants over time, ensuring the building can remain in use in the future (see Figure 3.3.2).

3.3.2 The pitched roof forms are exposed internally

ARTICULATING THE BUILDING FORM

The vernacular of the town is characterised by pitched slate roofs, deep window reveals, simple detailing and earthy brickwork. The new building uses this palette of materials to reflect this historic character but combines it with stripped-back, contemporary detailing. Perforated brickwork gables and low level curtain glazing are recessed with a brickwork frame, revealing their simple prismatic form. A crafted finish is brought to the elevations through projecting, tapering and hit-and-miss brickwork which breaks up larger expanses of brickwork (see Figure 3.3.3). A local buff tumbled brick was chosen with a varied colour and texture, meeting the aesthetic and performance requirements while also supporting the local economy.

Toward the car park, an open steel entrance canopy continues the pitched roof form at a smaller scale (see Figure 3.3.4). Window frames, delivery bay shutters, steelwork, external lights, bollards and escape doors are dark grey to match the dark slate roof tiles. Simple branding and signage support the elegance of the building. The design results in a bold contemporary building that embeds itself in a rich historic fabric, transforming an important gateway to the town centre.

3.3.3 Buff projecting brickwork is framed within an expressed gable

3.3.4 A lightweight steel canopy marks the entrance from the car park

CONCLUSION

The prevalent attitude of locating large retail stores in peripheral locations perpetuates decline in town centres. In the case of Northallerton, the loss of a key retail tenant would have had a negative impact on the high street. This ambitious project demonstrates how a major retail store can be integrated successfully into a historic town centre. While this approach comes with its challenges, the potential benefits of increased visitors, employment and the potential to rejuvenate the high street have far greater implications in creating thriving town centres.

TRANSFORMATIONS

- **Shopping in town**: the project keeps an important retailer in the heart of the town and demonstrates how the needs of retail tenants can be married with a contextual design response.

- **Brownfield site**: the new building gives a contemporary use to a brownfield site, extending the high street and creating a strong street presence where previously there was none.

- **Breaking up a large volume**: a large retail unit has been successfully integrated into the town through reference to the patterns evident in the historic grain and careful manipulation of the building form.

- **Contemporary detail**: the new building blends the character of the old town with a contemporary form and simple detailing, creating a bold but sensitive addition to the town.

CREDITS

Client: Jomast Developments

Architects: GT3 Architects

Contractor: Jomast Developments

Structural engineers: BGP Consulting Engineers

Landscape architects: Colour UDL

Planning consultancy: Nathaniel Lichfield & Partners Ltd

M&E engineers: Hill Lawrence Group

Awards: RIBA Yorkshire Award 2017; Brick Awards 2017, commended

Location: Westport, Co. Mayo, Ireland

Population: 6,198

Contract value: €3.8m

Status: Completed 2017

In many places, services such as schools and medical centres have relocated to the edge of towns. Scoil Phádraig National School, in the heart of Co. Mayo's heritage town of Westport, demonstrates how a substantial new school building can be integrated into the heart of a town, supporting community life.

3.4.0 The school and church seen from across the town

SITE AND CONTEXT

Westport, situated on Clew Bay on the Atlantic coast, is one of Ireland's few planned towns. In the 1700s an original village of around 700 people was cleared to make way for new gardens for Westport House, the stately home of the Marquess of Sligo. To rehouse workers and tenants, a new town named Westport was created by architect William Leeson, which prospered as a centre for linen and cotton in the 1800s. Located amongst a series of low drumlins, it is characterised by a series of urban set pieces built in a Georgian style along medieval urban design principles. At its low-lying centre, tree-lined boulevards flank the channelled Carrowbeg River, fronted by narrow buildings typical of many Irish town centres. Steep streets fall from the surrounding landscape toward the river. Buildings are generally two and three storey with stone or stucco façades and Georgian proportions. While the heritage centre of the town has been little altered and new buildings have been sensitively integrated, a building boom over the past two decades has put pressure on its edges and seen the development of suburban housing along the main routes into town.

The merger of the Convent of Mercy girls' school and the Christian Brothers' boys' primary school offered the opportunity to create a new school building embedded in the heart of the town. The site itself was somewhat awkward, a deep but irregular plot with a narrow street frontage. It had the added constraint of building next to the protected Holy Trinity Church, a large Gothic-style church built in the nineteenth century. The design proposal by SJK Architects had to resolve safe access for pedestrians and vehicles. Adjacent to the town's pedestrian and cycle greenway, it offered an opportunity to connect into a network of safe, car-free routes around the town and potentially reduce car use.

ORGANISATION AND FORM

The new building is composed to respond to its sensitive context and integrate a substantial new building into the fabric of the town. The school is orthogonally aligned with the adjacent church (see Figure 3.4.1). A brick pedestrian walkway leads alongside the churchyard to a new public yard, framed between the church and single-storey perimeter wall to the school. The space creates opportunities for pupils and parents to meet and for civic activities to take place. The school hall, which is used both by the school and for community activities, articulates a public presence facing this yard. Opalescent clerestory windows rise above a rendered perimeter wall, expressing the height of the hall, while raised render lettering announces the name of the school below (see Figure 3.4.2). Punching through the white rendered perimeter wall, the brick walkway continues to a recessed entrance and through to an outdoor play yard framed by the classrooms and hall.

'When you walk through the doors of our new school for the first time, you get a magical feeling.'

School pupil, 6th Class

The building form is composed of two parts: a two-storey linear block to the north, separating vehicle access from pedestrians, and a single-storey pitched roof block enclosing a south facing courtyard (see Figure 3.4.3). The northern two-storey block houses ten classrooms. A spine of service spaces line the northern edge of the building, enabling classrooms to predominantly face south. A single-storey block wraps the west and south of the play yard with six classrooms. Mono-pitch roofs fall towards the courtyard, reducing the scale of the blocks and maximising light to the children's play yard (see Figure 3.4.4).

3.4.1 The new school is oriented to align with the adjacent Holy Trinity Church

3.4.2 A brick pathway leads to the school entrance, announced by the glazed school hall and raised lettering

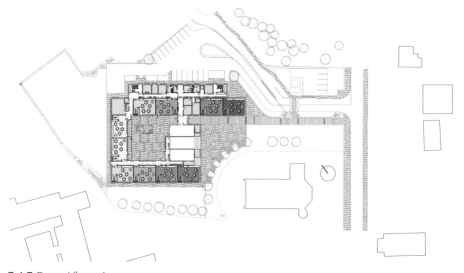

3.4.3 Ground floor plan

3.4.4 The play yard, flanked by single-storey and two-storey classroom blocks

Around the building, traffic routes are separated from pedestrian and cycle routes, which connect into the nearby greenway to promote active travel. In keeping the school in the town rather than relocating to the outskirts where land is more plentiful and potentially cheaper, the majority of pupils can walk or cycle to the school, thereby reducing traffic and car use. Staff parking is provided to the north of the site to the rear of the two-storey element and a number of drop-off zones for those needing vehicle access are arranged on the building side of moving traffic to minimise risk of collisions.

MATERIAL AND DETAIL

The new school has a restrained material palette befitting its sensitive setting. An ashlar limestone plinth recalls the low plinths typical of buildings around the town; this serves to anchor the building in its site and link the new building to the stone church. Above, white render continues to a datum, above which zinc standing seam cladding wraps the pitched roofs. Classrooms are glazed with a large window with a golden section proportion between fixed and opening elements, framing the church and town beyond. The rhythm of classrooms is subtly expressed through the location of dark grey downpipes on their dividing lines, breaking up the expanse of white render.

The classrooms are given a sense of individuality in a move which connects the school to the town's varied and vibrant shop fronts and the stained-glass church windows. Each has a distinct colour which is carried through the floor finish, joinery, shop-front doors, benches

3.4.5 Each classroom has a recognisable colour scheme, creating a strong sense of identity

and window reveals (*see* Figure 3.4.5). While common areas are subtly coloured, elements of each class's colour scheme carry through to the wayfinding, corridor ceilings and hall. Externally, the colours are expressed in window linings and panels and appear as coloured bands in the paving and yards, creating a sense of belonging, linking children to their classroom and the town.

The two yards are designed as a simple grid created by cast-in drainage channels, marbles and coloured bands. In the play yard, a sunken amphitheatre space is created with a low timber enclosure, creating opportunities for different types of outdoor play.

'It's so cool, it's so colourful and it has super links to the greenway… . The views are stunning… . There is an intercom so Mr Seoighe can speak to us… . I would rate the school more than 10 out of 10. I love it so much!'

School pupil, 4th Class

CONCLUSION

While the location for this new school in town posed difficult design challenges – most notably the location next to the protected church and resolving access to the site – the end result is a carefully composed major new community resource embedded in the town core. With the current tendency to consolidate and relocate facilities such as schools and medical facilities to the outskirts, Scoil Phádraig demonstrates the positive value of maintaining education within the centre of a town where it can become the heart of a community.

TRANSFORMATIONS
- **A new school in town**: a major new building has been integrated into the heart of historic town alongside the church. Keeping the school in town enables it to remain an important part of the community it serves.

- **Connections**: the building encourages active travel through new pedestrian routes connecting to the town's greenway. A new public yard between the church and the publicly accessible school hall invites the public onto the school site, making it part of the wider townscape.

- **Material simplicity**: a restrained material palette of render, zinc and stone draws from the character of the wider town to create a calm but contemporary addition, which integrates with the sensitive town fabric.

CREDITS
Client: Board of Management Scoil Phádraig

Architect: SJK Architects

Clerk of Works: Seán Quinn

Main contractor: Burns Construction and Civil Engineering

Quantity surveyor: Kane Crowe Kavanagh

M&E consultant: Patrick McCaul Associates

Civil and structural engineer: RPS Consulting Engineers

Project supervisor design process: OLM

Awards: RIAI Best Education Award 2018; RIAI Public Choice Award 2018, runner-up; Mies van der Rohe Award 2019, nominated

3.5 HEBDEN BRIDGE TOWN HALL, HEBDEN BRIDGE

Location: Hebden Bridge, West Yorkshire, UK

Population: 4,500

Contract value: £4m

Status: Completed 2012

In 2010 the town hall in Hebden Bridge became one of the first to be handed into community ownership and demonstrates what can be achieved when a community coalesces around a common vision.

3.5.0 The town hall seen from across the town

SITE AND CONTEXT

Located in the Upper Calder Valley, the West Yorkshire town of Hedben Bridge is nestled within a steep valley at the junction of the Calder and Hebden rivers. Little more than a hamlet before the 1850s, the town grew rapidly during industrialisation, profiting from the wool trade and its links to Manchester and Leeds. Large mills grew at the confluence of the rivers where they could benefit from transport links and power drawn from fast-flowing streams. With the decline of industry in the mid-twentieth century, the town developed a lively alternative scene which increased its popularity as a tourist destination. Since the 1990s it has grown as a dormitory settlement due to its proximity to neighbouring cities but has continued to prosper as a centre for independent shops, businesses and cafés.

The project site is located in the heart of the conservation area and consists of a number of buildings. The Grade II listed town hall, a flamboyant late Victorian stone building dating from 1897, is located at the southern end of the market place overlooking Hebden Water. Adjacent is the fire station (1898) which appears as part of the same building, despite its later construction. Alongside the river, a plain stone transmission station and a 1970s link building enjoy views over Hebden Water. The northern portion of the site was given over to car parking over two levels, following the fall of the site toward the water.

COMMUNITY OWNERSHIP

Once it had been transferred to community ownership in 2010, the Hebden Bridge Community Association was established to run the town hall in public ownership and ensure its place at the heart of civic life. This required widening participation in the town hall, enabling its full occupation and extending its use. The association developed a brief that could generate enough revenue to sustain the long-term future of the town hall as the heart of local democratic processes and decision-making. The aim was to create a hub for local services and information, offer accessible space for hire and support local enterprise. A brief for a sustainable mix of uses was developed consisting of a series of new lettable workspace units in addition to those already existing in the town hall, alongside community provision including a 200-seat conference room, two seminar rooms and smaller meeting rooms. The brief and the subsequent design proposals were developed through extensive community engagement, including a number of day-long events, school activities, a website, online polls and voting on case study examples.

RESOLVING SITE COMPLEXITIES

The project evolved from a number of design priorities which addressed accessibility, townscape and functional aspects of the proposal. Through extensive testing of the building form and local consultation, the transmission station and later extension along the river were demolished. This allowed a south-facing public courtyard to be created on the riverside, as well as allowing good views out of the buildings to the river and views into the site from the surrounding areas. The new building reinstates a three-storey edge to Hangingroyd Road to the north, reinforcing the historic fabric of the town and wrapping around the courtyard to the west where it steps down toward the water (see Figure 3.5.1). The roof form is a three-pitched gable, keeping the ridge heights low and responding to the form of the town hall. This linear block extends to the corner of the site facing the market, where its gabled form extends the form of the town hall to cleanly address the market place, emphasising its civic importance (see Figure 3.5.2).

3.5.1 The new three-gabled wing encloses a central courtyard

3.5.2 The new gable connecting to the existing town hall creates a civic presence on the market place

As it was constructed in several stages, the circulation, legibility and levels of the existing building were complex. The new main entrance is through the arched gateway of the fire station opposite the market place. This leads into a main foyer which opens into a café lounge, beyond which is a 200-seat conference hall overlooking Hebden Water. Secondary entrances from the north are narrow and designed to be a similar scale to the ginnels or alleys common around the town. The majority of circulation takes place around the courtyard, helping with orientation and creating a sense of openness. The uses of the building change from public at ground floor level to more private enterprise space and offices above.

SIMPLE FORMS AND DETAILS

The town has a rich palette of materials but is dominated by stone buildings. The town hall itself is made of richly decorated stonework; the new building reflects this language but strips back the decoration to avoid pastiche. This is combined with moments of contemporary material and detail, for example the standing seam metal wrap around the conference hall which folds to become a terrace over the water (see Figure 3.5.3). Crisply detailed stonework with simple punched windows openings are composed to echo the shape and organisation of the town hall fenestration. Windows are often in pairs or threes with narrow stone mullions, a contemporary interpretation of the late Victorian window details. At courtyard level windows and doors are timber, softening the edges of the new public space. Above they are dark grey, with metal brise soleil above the south-facing opening to prevent overheating (see Figure 3.5.4). The pitched roofs are slate clad to match the town hall and include large areas of photovoltaic and solar thermal panels to reduce running costs.

3.5.3 The conference room overlooks Hebden Water

3.5.4 Stripped-back stone detailing contrasts with the ornate original building

CONCLUSION

The new town hall has quickly become an important part of the community, no more so than during the 2015 Boxing Day floods. With the Calder River peaking at 3.5m above its usual zenith, much of the centre of Hebden Bridge was flooded and the town hall became a crisis response centre. With only minor basement flooding and with one of the few working broadband connections, the building became a focal point for relief efforts and a place where people could congregate as well as supplying food and drink. The town hall became a centre for the community and has grown into its civic role, changing perceptions about what such a building is for, how it can become a centre of community life and how a community can take control of its assets to create meaningful change.

TRANSFORMATIONS

- **Community-led**: as one of the first community asset transfers of a town hall, the development has led the way in considering what a town hall is for and how it can be used.

- **Civic role**: the town hall has been designed to enable a range of uses from community oriented activity to supporting local enterprise and businesses.

- **Creating a heart**: re-orienting the building by removing the transformer station has created a sheltered south-facing public heart to the building overlooking the river.

- **Scale and form**: the scale of the building has been carefully designed to fit the scale of the town and to interpret the scale, form and language of the town hall to create a continuity with the listed building.

CREDITS

Client: Hebden Bridge Community Association

Architect: Bauman Lyons Architects

Structural Engineering and M&E: ARUP

Contractor: STG

Location: Bishop Auckland, County Durham, UK

Population: 25,455

Contract value: £2.5m

Status: Completed 2018

A bold building on a prominent site set in the heart of a historic town centre declares the ambition for Bishop Auckland – home to one of the most important and best-preserved medieval bishops' palaces in all of Europe – to become a major new tourist destination.

3.6.0 The welcome building completes a formerly derelict corner of the market place

SITE AND CONTEXT

Bishop Auckland is a major market town located between Darlington and Durham in north-east England. Its history is intertwined with the Prince Bishops of Durham who held the lands around the town from the tenth century. With industrialisation in the nineteenth century, the town became a major coal mining and railway hub, and expanded rapidly. The prosperity of the town peaked in this period; during the twentieth century the decline of coal mining and railway closures resulted in major loss of employment, compounded by the decline of the service and retail sectors. The town continues to exhibit higher than average levels of unemployment.

In an attempt to help address these issues a regeneration charity, The Auckland Project, is working to create a new visitor destination in Bishop Auckland, using art, faith and heritage to fuel long-term change and revitalisation. It began in 2012 with the purchase of Auckland Castle and a series of paintings by the Spanish artist Francisco de Zurbarán by financier Jonathan Ruffer, who founded The Auckland Project (then known as Auckland Castle Trust) with the aim of making the paintings and castle accessible to visitors, who in turn would contribute to the regeneration of the town. Since then, the project has grown into a multi-faceted visitor destination and works directly with the local community to make beautiful experiences and opportunities accessible to everyone. The destination itself will be made up of seven linked developments. A purpose-built welcome centre (the Auckland Tower), a mining art gallery in a converted historic building in the town centre and a deer park are already open to visitors, and Auckland Castle re-opened in November 2019 after a three-year conservation programme. In the coming years there will also be a Walled Garden, complete with its own restaurant, a new build Faith Museum and a Spanish Gallery due for completion (see Figure 3.6.1). Almost £150m has already been committed to The Auckland Project to date, with support from a wide range of organisations and charitable trusts, including The National Lottery Heritage Fund. The charity is also working closely with a range of partners to encourage investment in Bishop Auckland and its infrastructure, supporting projects such as the Heritage Action Zones to renovate historic buildings in disrepair and the refurbishment of the market place.

Auckland Tower was the second Auckland Project site to reach completion and the first to be purpose built. The Auckland Project's vision was that the new building should be a first port of call for visitors, an orientation point that would signpost visitors to the various attractions as well as being an attraction in itself. The project developed through extensive engagement with local residents, the County Council and English Heritage to ensure the design was sensitive to its conservation area setting.

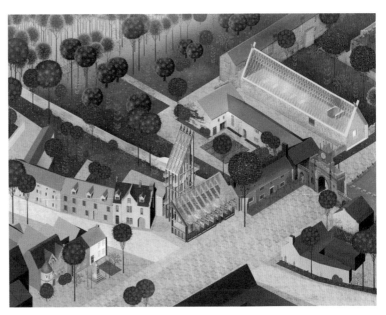

3.6.1 Collage image of the welcome building showing the square and clock tower with the Scotland Gallery refurbishment in the background

A TOWER AND A HALL

The building provides visitor information, a ticketing hall, a versatile exhibition and events space, and WCs plus a 29-m viewing tower with a 15-m high viewing platform offering panoramic views across the town, deer park and the landscape beyond. It is composed as an ensemble of three timber structures with different characters which enclose an inner courtyard. The building is entered under a lightweight tower which is set back from the street, creating an informal forecourt. An open skeletal timber frame – a metaphorical siege engine breaking down the walls between the castle and the town – encases a concrete lift shaft wrapped by a staircase which connects a series of theatrical viewing balconies overlooking the castle and town (see Figure 3.6.2). This tower complements a series of historic spires in the town centre and is designed to be a visible marker from the landscape and streetscape. Careful exploration of the form through townscape views and vistas was prepared to assess the visual impact of the tower and ensure its height and proportion sat comfortably in the context.

The welcome and ticketing hall is a more substantial feeling two-storey timber building reminiscent of a market hall. It creates a strong edge to the market place and frames views toward the clock tower, a gateway to the historic approach to the castle. Rather than following the curve of the original site, the building form extends the building line of the adjacent college buildings (see Figures 3.6.3 and 3.6.4). As an urban design strategy this presents the gable of the Auckland Tower to the market place,

3.6.2 Timber model of the proposal showing the contrast between the tower and the hall

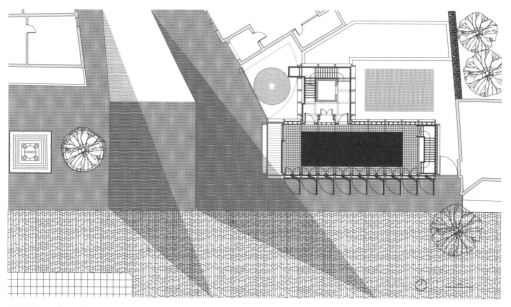

3.6.3 First floor plan

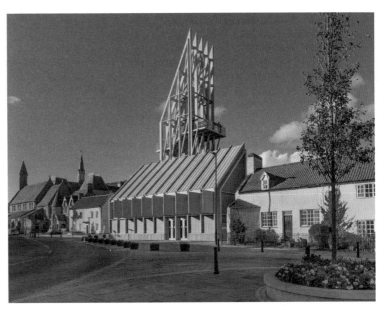

3.6.4 The welcome hall continues the edge to the market place

announcing its presence. The roof negotiates between the adjacent buildings and the eaves continue that of the college buildings while the pitch rises to a ridge matching the adjoining Dutch gabled townhouse, creating a dialogue with these two neighbouring buildings. Entered under the tower from the market place, the building contains a reception, small shop and ticketing desk located at ground floor level and a space for education, interpretation and social functions, decorated with painted motifs, above. Across an inner courtyard, a single-storey ancillary block on the northern part of the site contains WCs and staff offices.

The positioning of the building was made possible by the realignment of Bishop Auckland market place, which was funded by the North East Local Enterprise Partnership and delivered by Durham County Council. New crossings were also introduced to better connect the market place to Auckland Tower and to the clock tower that marks the entrance to the castle.

NARRATIVE DETAILS
The building is designed to respond to the history of the site and the fantastical narrative environment of the bishop's castle. Extensive references to paintings, drawings and texts about the site were made to understand how the site had evolved over time, from Roman fort to visitor attraction. While the building is secular, it borrows motifs and iconography from religious architecture.

A concrete plinth anchors the building to the ground. European Larch Glulam beams rise to create the ribbed structure of the building, finished with a light grey pigment to provide a decorative finish and protection to the timber. This is left open for the tower, allowing the winding stair and lift shaft to be seen through the structure, with perforated metal screens covering the roof. The welcome hall has a greater sense of presence; this solidity reinforces the street scene. Here, the timber ribs are infilled. The roof is a standing seam metal cladding sitting between the structural bays. At ground floor a fibre cement rainscreen bearing stencilled text describing the history of the town infills the frame (see Figure 3.6.5). The timber-lined exhibition space above has two treatments. To the north, profiled Larch fins filter daylight into the space. The south façade has two modes: open and closed. When closed, the hall has a simple volumetric form articulated by timber ribs, but when opened casement windows and shutters create a connection between the decorated hall and the market place. The gable of the welcome hall is fully glazed and looks down the market place, connecting visitors back to the wider town (see Figure 3.6.6)

3.6.5 Stencilled text around the base of the centre describes the history of the town

3.6.6 The exhibition space looks down the market place, framed through the glazed gable

CONCLUSION

Auckland Tower is a prominent marker at the heart of the Bishop Auckland, a point of arrival, orientation and welcome for visitors. A contemporary interpretation of a market hall and siege tower, the building sits sensitively within the scale and form of the conservation area and draws on the fantastical narrative and history of the town to inform its design. As the first purpose-built building completed for the Auckland Trust, Auckland Tower announces the trust's ambition for the long-term heritage and tourism-led transformation of the town.

TRANSFORMATIONS

- **A visible marker**: the tower creates a marker visible from the landscape and within the town centre, drawing people to the heart of the town.

- **Townscape**: the building scape carefully responds to its surroundings, completing a vacant plot. By breaking the boundary of the site, the building gable announces itself on approach to the market place.

- **Public spaces**: the building strengthens the market place, reinforcing its edge and realigning traffic routes to create improved opportunities for people to gather. Recessing the tower creates a new entrance yard and separates this from a public courtyard within.

- **Narrative**: the building draws on the rich stories and heritage of the castle to inform the materials, decoration and finishes of the new building.

CREDITS

Client: The Auckland Trust

Architect: Niall McLaughlin Architects

Main contractor: VEST Construction

Project management: Turner & Townsend

M&E consultant: TGA

Structural engineer: The Moreton Partnership

Awards: RTPI Award for Planning Excellence, Excellence in Planning for Heritage and Culture category, finalist

CHAPTER 4

Public Spaces: Encouraging Social Life

4.1 THE VALUE OF PUBLIC SPACE

Public space is a vital part of the experience of a place: the street we use to get to work or to the shops, the parks where people play sports or walk dogs, the playgrounds where children play, the paths where we bump into friends, and the squares where a community comes together for festivities and markets. While the streetscape is a first impression of the town for residents and visitors, it is vitally important as a social space of meeting and encounter. One of the greatest legacies of European urbanisation is the traditional market square or piazza. Surrounded by buildings and at the meeting point of important streets, these enclosed spaces are the social heart of towns. Multifunctional spaces for economic and social activity, they are places of exchange of goods, ideas, politics and debate,[1] the focus of the rhythms and rituals of everyday life.

Physical spaces are vital in promoting a sense of belonging and well-being. A well-designed, managed and maintained streetscape has many positive benefits:

- increasing footfall within town centres, supporting local businesses
- encouraging conviviality, informal meeting and socialising
- promoting healthy lifestyles by encouraging people to spend time outdoors, and
- creating a sense of belonging.

BALANCING MOVEMENT AND CIRCULATION

Today there is often limited variety and frequency of community interaction in public spaces due to the impact of vehicles in places often not designed to cope with the weight of traffic. Design frequently comes second to considerations of movement and control of vehicles,[2] and when change occurs it is often in response to traffic management and the infrastructure required by the car. Prime areas of public realm can be saturated with parking and congested with traffic, with all the negatives this brings: pollution, barriers to movement, noise and loss of space for people. The competing demands of events, parking, pedestrians, vehicles, shops, cafés, monuments, seating and planting can in some instances lead to confusing and contradictory spaces. Accommodating sufficient parking space and ever-larger number of vehicles in smaller communities presents a challenge to the compactness and perceived quietness that makes them attractive places in which to live.[3]

Improving public transport seems an obvious change to combat car use but the small populations of many rural towns affects the viability of public transport systems.[4] Creating appealing cost-effective links between places to work, shop and live is a challenge for policymakers in the face of the freedom of personal mobility provided by the car. Recent policy changes, for example those developed through the 'Manual for Streets', aim to redress the balance between the vehicle, pedestrian and cyclists. This can increase social interaction, revitalise trade and reduce accidents.[5] Equally, this suggests streets as places for people to inhabit and enjoy rather than spaces dominated by the car.

VIBRANT PUBLIC SPACES

Squares and market places were historically the focus of social activities, followed by streets, lanes and green spaces around them. Well-designed and maintained public spaces, particularly those that relate to landscape and heritage, are an important aspect of local character. Streets, squares, parks, gardens, allotments, outdoor sports facilities, civic spaces, market places, pedestrian areas, green corridors and play areas all have different characters and attract different groups of people. Their character is influenced by a complex mix of factors: proportion, width, materials, planting, the rhythm of façades, occupancy, use, the amount of space for vehicles and pedestrians and quality of street furniture.[6] Connections between different spaces for pedestrian, vehicle, bicycle and public transport are also important to their success. If a sequence of spaces is high quality and safe, it is more likely to be used by pedestrians and more likely to encourage people to linger.

Of those surveyed by CABE, 85% feel that the quality of public space and the built environment have a direct impact on the way they feel.[7] Places with high-quality public spaces can attract economic investment and are seen as good places to live and work. Green spaces and planting are widely recognised to have positive health benefits and play a vital role in countering climate change and encouraging biodiversity, social interaction, exercise and play. Furthermore, children socialise better where there are good places to play outdoors.[8] Some towns have created distinctiveness through the innovative use of green spaces, such as Todmorden in Yorkshire, the home of Incredible Edible. This community movement aims to make the town self-sufficient by using leftover public spaces to grow and share food, creating a green route through the town that highlights the importance of biodiversity and small-scale food production.

The design of public spaces from their overall character down to the smallest detail is vital in how people perceive them. Condition and upkeep have a huge impact on their appearance and they can often become cluttered with unnecessary signage and road markings or distressed through wear and tear. Shared materials or street furniture can lend a sense of continuity, while the unexpected unfolding of views and vistas and changing visual juxtapositions create a sense of anticipation and enjoyment as people move around, as described so well by Gorden Cullen.[9] Use of colour to enliven dull buildings, introducing planting and coordinating quality street furniture can all enhance the quality of public spaces.

COLLABORATION AND 'JOINING THE DOTS'

Rethinking public spaces needs the input of a variety of stakeholders and public bodies. Open and exploratory design processes with local people can encourage the re-thinking of the purpose of underused and unloved public spaces. Through collaboration between community groups, artists, performers, local people and architects, scales of project from updates to street furniture, pocket parks to major transformation changes can be created alongside local people. In many places creating opportunities to rebalance priorities for vehicles, pedestrians and cyclists can have a transformative effect on the social life of small places. Creating new connections through high-quality public spaces can create a new focus for civic life – places people enjoy and spend time in. Holistic design thinking led by architects and designers can create opportunities out of highways improvement and drainage works – 'joining the dots' as the example of Clonakilty 400 demonstrates. New public spaces can create links to heritage and history, and the involvement of artists and creative practitioners can lead to imaginative responses to local stories, histories and narratives. The following projects illustrate how connected thinking, listening to the voices of local people and considering the wider impact of a scheme, alongside creative thinking and imagination, can transform public spaces into the spaces of opportunity, social life and belonging.

4.2 BRIDGE STREET, CALLAN

Location: Callan, Co. Kilkenny, Ireland

Population: 2,330

Status: Ongoing

The Bridge Street Project is one part of a long-term collective re-imagining of the future of Upper Bridge Street, Callan, Co. Kilkenny. Developed through interdisciplinary collaboration between theatre-makers, architecture practitioners, residents, business owners and the wider community of Callan, the project explores the role of the high street as a collective civic space.

4.2.0 'Bridge Street Will Be' performance

SITE AND CONTEXT

Callan is a medieval market town with over 800 years of history located 16 km south of Kilkenny, Ireland. The town has become of a focus for artistic activity with many arts organisations and practices relocating or being set up over the past decade, joining the established KCAT Arts Centre, a pioneering inclusive arts centre within a European context.[10] A number of these organisations have been exploring the future of Upper Bridge Street, a narrow curving street connecting the King's River to the main crossroads. Historically the town's market street, it was a bustling centre with pubs, groceries, a drapers, funeral home and bakeries. However, increasing levels of traffic congestion during the twentieth century supressed this vibrancy and from the 1980s businesses started to relocate to the much wider Green Street. By the time the Callan bypass was built in 1997, the upper street had fallen into dereliction. Some façades were lost to redevelopment while others were hollowed out to make space for new projects that never materialised.

ENGAGEMENT PROCESS

For some years one-off art events and residencies have been run in Callan linked to Abhainn Rí Festival, a Community Festival of Participation and Inclusion initiated by Callan Community Network. 'Commonage' invited designers and architects to Callan for a series of design and build summer schools over the summers of 2010–13, inspired by a project by Japanese artist Tadashi Kawamata's work in the French village of Saint-Thélo. The projects built on the town's assets and skills (such as local carpenters) to develop inclusive decision-making processes involving participants across generations and abilities in the creation of temporary interventions in the public realm. These summer schools led to the town's involvement in 'Forecast', a project commissioned by Kilkenny Leader Partnership and Kilkenny County Council Forward Planning Department, exploring participatory planning in five towns in the county. Callan's chosen theme was 'Move', and London-based Studio Weave was appointed to explore how children navigated through the town. Bridge Street was closed for a day for 'Children at Play', an event featuring chalk games, food, live music and a children's disco (see Figure 4.2.1). Over 300 people attended, demonstrating Bridge Street's potential as a site around which the community could come together to consider urban renewal.

4.2.1 'Children at Play', a day of activities exploring the potential of Bridge Street as a public space

Around the same time, members of Equinox Theatre, an inclusive theatre company based at KCAT, were concerned about the accessibility of the street, in particular for people with impaired mobility. During the 2014 Abhainn Rí Festival, a pop-up café was opened in a disused shop front on Bridge Street to open a conversation with the community to explore these issues. Local people were invited to share stories about the street over a cup of tea, from which emerged the idea of developing a theatre script made up of local stories. Collaborators were gathered and the theatre piece developed with writer John Morton and director Donal Gallagher. The two disciplines, architecture and theatre, were responding independently to similar issues with the shared goal of re-imagining the town's civic spaces. Funding from an Arts Council Arts Participation Project Award and a Kilkenny County Council Arts Act Grant enabled a collaboration between the Workhouse Union team and Equinox Theatre under the umbrella Trasna Productions.

THE BRIDGE STREET PROJECT

The resulting Bridge Street Project combined a theatre production, 'Bridge Street Will Be', and an architectural intervention, 'Reflected Elevation'. The theatre strand focused on performance-based civic participation and engagement with the internal spaces of the street while the architectural strand would address the regeneration of the outside spaces through bottom-up community workshops. The aim was to respond to the people as well as the dilapidated buildings that make up Bridge Street and transform it, even temporarily, back into the heart of the town.

Over three weeks, Studio Weave ran a series of workshops, Bridge Street: MAKE, exploring the ornate traditional façades found in Callan. Extensive groundwork was carried out developing connections, gaining access to buildings and garnering support from local businesses and homeowners. Over 50 participants gave up their evenings to join workshops to paint the façades of the buildings in a paintscape representing the various lives of the street and capturing the many changes to its buildings (see Figures 4.2.2 and 4.2.3). Closing the street for a few hours every day to paint formed a new public realm, created chance meetings and allowed local people to admire the beauty of the buildings. While the closures were the main source of disruption for the wider community, it was this disruption that led to the engagement of residents who may not otherwise have taken part.

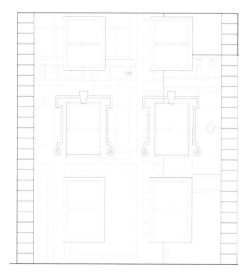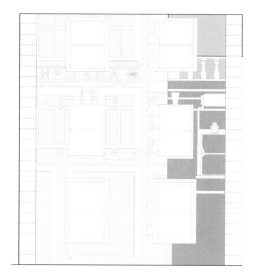

——— Existing facade features

——— New painted facade features

Approximate facade surface area: 30sqm

4.2.2 'Reflected Elevation', a paintscape representing the various lives of the street

4.2.3 The final paintscape was painted by local people over a series of evening workshops

Alongside the paintscape workshops, Studio Weave and a local carpenter ran daily workshops to create a series of lightweight timber cubes to act as public furniture (see Figure 4.2.4). These acted as seating for the theatre performance but they can also be combined in different ways to suit different needs and have been retained as a community resource for future activities. These two elements became the stage set for the performance and a lasting legacy of the project which remains visible to residents and passers-by today.

From the stories collected by the Equinox Theatre Company, local theatre-maker John Morton created a script woven from local legends and oral histories. A cast of over 80 community and professional actors, led by Equinox Theatre and Asylum Productions, unfolded their stories using the street and its buildings as their stage in an immersive theatre production. The audience was allowed to wander freely in and out of buildings and through the street, rediscovering this overlooked part of the town (see Figure 4.2.5). By its second night the show was sold out for the rest of the week, with many people coming back for a second and third performance.

4.2.4 Creating public furniture for the performance

4.2.5 The immersive theatre production using Bridge Street as a stage

PHASE 2

The following year, Studio Weave returned to the town for 'Courtyard Screen', a project to create a shared outdoor space at Fennelly's, an experimental cultural venue on Bridge Street. This set out to create a new civic space for people to gather and to develop a shared vision for the renewal of Bridge Street (*see* Figure 4.2.6). Through wood-carving, turning and sewing workshops a new canopy structure was built to host a pop-up cinema for the Abhainn Rí Festival in 2016. Over 120 participants took part in hands-on events exploring the future of the street. The outcomes of this project have fed into Callan's Local Area Plan 2019, which highlights Bridge Street as a critical area needing rejuvenation, and has led to funding as part of a pilot study to encourage more people to live in rural towns.

Workhouse Union has continued to explore how participatory spatial practice can explore how small towns are inhabited by different people and the future of these small places through artist and architectural residencies in Callan and the surrounding areas. These have included residencies by Spanish architectural collective Todo Por La Praxis, focused on the experience of young people and their sense of place and belonging within public space in a rural town, and *Town Traits: Alternative Census*, a photographic portrait of the town by artist Michelle Browne. Fennelly's of Callan has now established itself as a permanent café and cultural space in the town, serving rustic loaf from Keogh's Model Bakery – the last remaining traditional business on Lower Bridge Street.

4.2.6 'Courtyard Screen', Fennelly's

CONCLUSION

Through an innovative and collaborative approach to engaging with local people and small scale intervention, the projects in Callan demonstrate the value architects and designers can bring to rethinking public space in smaller settlements. Through hands-on performance and making, the sequence of projects have made positive transformations to the town and influenced long-term thinking about the town's future.

TRANSFORMATIONS

- **Collaboration:** collaboration between local organisations, residents, artists and architects has led to an inventive and innovative approach to rethinking the civic role of a neglected street.

- **Narrative and storytelling:** the use of local history and stories proved an effective way to engage local people in thinking about their place and future.

- **Raising profiles:** the project has resulted in a renewed interest in the town's public spaces and highlighted Bridge Street as a critical area for regeneration. Funding towards this has been sought through a government pilot scheme 'Town Centre Living Initiative' to rejuvenate rural towns by encouraging more people to live there.

- **Influencing policy:** the outcomes of the public engagement process led by Studio Weave through The Bridge Street Project and 'Courtyard Screen' have been incorporated into Callan's Local Area Plan 2019.

CREDITS

Architect: Studio Weave

Client: Trasna Productions

Civic engagement producers: Rosie Lynch, Etaoin Holahan

Commissioned by: Trasna Productions

Funders: Arts Council Kilkenny Leader Partnership

Theatre company: Equinox Theatre Company and Asylum Productions

Writer: John Morton

Location: Prescot, Merseyside, UK

Population: 11,184

Status: Completed 2019

The result of an RIBA competition, Prescot Forum transforms a neglected and underused public space into a new civic heart for the town. The project opens up a difficult to access site, makes new connections with the surrounding buildings and streets and creates a range of opportunities for social interaction. A flexible civic space overlooked by a pavilion created by reimagining a dilapidated toilet block creates an active social space at centre of the life of the town.

4.3.0: The Forum creates a new public space at the heart of the town

SITE AND CONTEXT
Prescot is one of the most historic market towns in Merseyside and dates from before the Norman conquest. Home to the first Elizabethan theatre outside London, its rich industrial past in coal mining, pottery and watch-making is displayed in its many historic buildings and features. With the decline of the twice weekly market in the early twentieth century, the town's market hall and town hall fell into disrepair and were eventually demolished as part of the clearance of Market Place in the 1960s. This also saw Georgian and Victorian houses to the north and shops to the west of the square demolished, while the southern side was redeveloped as a bus

station and car park. The square itself was made into a municipal open space with new grassed areas, flower beds, retaining walls, public conveniences and a limited amount of seating. Public events and markets shifted from the old market square to nearby streets pedestrianised in the 1980s, leaving the square devoid of activity and on the fringes of Prescott's civic life. High retaining walls and poor access isolated it from its surroundings. Materials were of poor quality and not suited to a conservation area, further exacerbated by removal of benches and the closure of the public toilets at the west of the site.

ENGAGEMENT PROCESS

Despite these failings, Market Place had potential to be reimagined as a central focus for the town. Major redevelopment is taking place with the aim of revitalising the town centre. These projects include a £3.2m Heritage Lottery funded Townscape Heritage Initiative (THI) which is refreshing historic shop fronts and public spaces, the construction of Shakespeare North Playhouse, a theatre and cultural venue to the north of the market place, the conversion of a shopping centre into a cinema and plans to revitalise the cemetery and churchyard.

The THI commissioned a public engagement process to establish what residents would like to see happen in the market place. Over a three-month period, Liverpool-based PLACED developed a brand, conducted workshops with schools and older residents, carried out a survey, ran family activities and ended with an exhibition aiming to engage as many people as possible. Popular aspirations included a sociable space (a destination with opportunities for shelter, markets, performances and evening activities), food and drink provision, and greening of the space.

An RIBA competition for the reimagining of Market Place as a focus for town life was launched in 2017. The aim was to create a landmark space that would be well used by the public day and night, was locally distinctive and supported, and connected to the wider economic and social activity of the town centre. The initial 42 entries were reduced to a shortlist of five and an overall winner was announced in Mark Wray Architects and SEED Landscape Design.

THE FORUM

The competition-winning proposal takes the idea of the Forum – defined as a place of business, meeting and exchange but also a meeting or medium for discussion – as a model for the market square. Removing barriers that isolated the existing space and establishing new connections to the cultural assets of the town aims to make the space a new focus and gathering space serving the different attractions and townspeople.

The Forum is designed to have a number of different characters. The wooded character of the churchyard and cemetery wraps around the eastern and southern sides, forming a green backdrop. Terraced steps flow out of these grassed areas, replacing obstructive retaining walls. These terraces are urban in character and are designed to connect the Forum to the theatre development (see Figure 4.3.1). Timber benches create opportunities for social interaction overlooking the event space below. South-facing sculptural grass terraces address changes in level in the foreground of the square.

4.3.1 The Forum deals with complex topography through a series of terraces

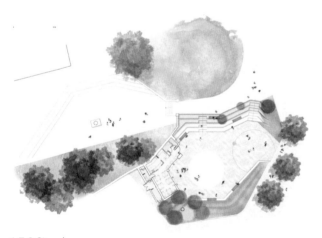

4.3.2 Site plan

The heart of the Forum is a flexible civic space which makes use of the most level part of the site (see Figure 4.3.2). Accessed from the north through two sets of steps and with level access from the east on one of the only level parts of the site, this circular space is designed to maximise flexibility to allow for a variety of different uses throughout the year. Yorkstone paving and setts create a high quality and durable finish which ties in with the surrounding historic context (see Figure 4.3.3).

4.3.3 Materials such as Yorkstone setts, precast stone and integrated lighting give a high-quality finish to the new public space

4.3.4 The pavilion embedded in the slope of the site

THE PAVILION

A new public pavilion is created by repurposing the existing public conveniences as a space to provide shelter and a destination. The intervention responds to the importance of the war memorial and church with a low-key response that does not compete with these monuments but is embedded in the slope of the site. The building is anchored into the site by the green backdrop which provides separation between houses to the south and the public square (*see* Figure 4.3.4).

The existing brick public conveniences are retained and extended to wrap around the central event space. Where new openings are created, precast stone is used to create post and lintel frames, and full-height glazing folds away to merge inside and outside, blurring the boundary between the pavilion and event space.

The pavilion has potential to be run by the community for educational, arts and social events or as a café while retaining separate access to public toilets. Facilities have been provided to allow for temporary structures and events to host a range of different activities to provide an ongoing and varied programme

4.3.5 The Forum has already hosted a series of public activities, such as an ice rink

4.3.6 The Forum's opening night

within the space. Despite only completing in November 2019, the space has already hosted an ice rink, lantern parade and music performances, and a year-round programme of events is planned (see Figures 4.3.5 and 4.3.6).

CONCLUSION

The reimagining of the former Market Place creates a multifunctional social space at the heart of the town, a forum for local people. It removes existing barriers and connects the space into the life of the town, making new connections to the church and wider public spaces and buildings. It makes use of complex topography to create a variety of places for people to sit and engage with the Forum and its activities. Reconnecting the space to its surroundings by removing high retaining walls and opening up the site brings it back into the social life of the town. The Forum is already becoming part of the rhythm of the town's life, hosting events and community activities at the site of the historic market place.

TRANSFORMATIONS

- **The Forum:** the project creates a new civic space where the local community can come together to meet, talk, observe and take part in the life of the town.

- **Creative adaptation:** the existing public conveniences has been repurposed and extended, creating a community space and café to care for the Forum and to curate activities and events.

- **New connections:** the space has been opened up and barriers that previously isolated it have been removed, creating a new flexible civic gathering space to serve the local community.

- **Level changes:** the change in level across the site has been harnessed to create a range of opportunities for sitting and an amphitheatre.

CREDITS

Client: Prescot Town Heritage Initiative

Architect: Mark Wray Architects

Landscape architect: SEED Landscape Design

Structural engineer: Momentum Consulting Engineers

Quantity surveyor: Howard Grady Associates

4.4 HELENSBURGH TOWN CENTRE, HELENSBURGH

Location: Helensburgh, Argyll and Bute, Scotland, UK

Population: 15,430

Status: Completed 2015

The redevelopment of Colquhoun Square, the esplanade and surrounding streets creates a connected, high-quality public realm focused on the pedestrian. Creating new spaces to sit, meet, interact, conduct business and access services supports the everyday life of the town, creating a new civic heart in an area previously dominated by traffic.

4.4.0 Colquhoun Square, the centrepiece of the public realm redevelopment

SITE AND CONTEXT

Helensburgh is a Victorian town located 40 km north-west of Glasgow on the north bank of the River Clyde. Receiving its burgh charter in 1802, the town is largely a product of new forms of transport emerging in the Victorian era. Initially, paddle steamers brought tourists up the Clyde, while later the arrival of the railway led to the growth of the commute to Glasgow and Edinburgh. The older heart of the town is laid out on a planned grid system with wide elegant avenues, a long seafront promenade and a number of Victorian parks and gardens. Later development up the slopes behind the town include Charles Rennie Macintosh's Hill House.

The Scottish government has invested widely in improvements to the quality of the environment in town centres to encourage sustainable economic regeneration. The ambitious regeneration plan for Helensburgh, part of the Argyll and Bute Council CHORD initiative (Campbeltown, Helensburgh, Oban, Rothesay, Dunoon), aimed to improve economic activity in the town and enhance the visitor experience. The council hoped to raise the competitiveness of the town as a place to invest, enhance local character, increase visitor numbers, reduce traffic congestion and improve parking provision. The project focused on the redesign of Colquhoun Square, which had a high proportion of road space, alongside the redevelopment of the principal surrounding streets and the West Bay Esplanade (*see* Figure 4.4.1).

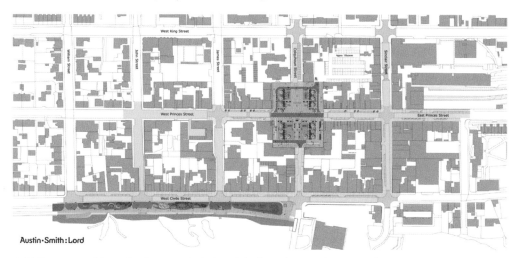

4.4.1 The extent of the redevelopment, including Colquhoun Square, the surrounding streets and the esplanade

ENGAGEMENT PROCESS

The design team took an evidence-based approach, scoping out and refocusing the project through extensive engagement to establish what would have the biggest positive impact on the community. A 20-month engagement period consisted of walks, on-street consultation, public exhibitions, design workshops, an online ideas bank, outdoor 'gazebo days', walking and talking events with local historians, 'stickering' plans and engagement with 260 pupils from local schools through 'My Creative Community Day'. Over 100 community and civic groups were consulted and the feedback was collated into a Statement of Participation demonstrating how the engagement and collaboration fed into the design proposal. The engagement particularly identified an interest in future whole-town events, such as an ice rink, markets, fireworks displays and winter festivals, and an aspiration for a new museum for local residents and visitors. Proposals were tested and refined through this engagement process, ensuring support from local people and businesses.

BALANCING TRAFFIC AND PEDESTRIAN PRIORITIES

Colquhoun Square was dominated by a major crossroad which divided the space. The implementation of a sustainable traffic management system aimed to reduce traffic through the town centre. The extent of road space and pedestrian space has been reassigned to centre a major public space which celebrates and strengthens the town's grid pattern (see Figure 4.4.2). Car parking has been reorganised, footway widths increased and road crossing distances reduced to assist pedestrian movement. Paths, soft landscaped areas, lines of trees and lighting columns are organised on a simple grid system, enhancing the setting of a number of high-quality listed buildings around the square. The square was planted with 16 large, semi-mature trees to reinforce the Helensburgh tradition of planting cherry blossom trees along the street grid network, reinforcing and extending the town's existing identity.

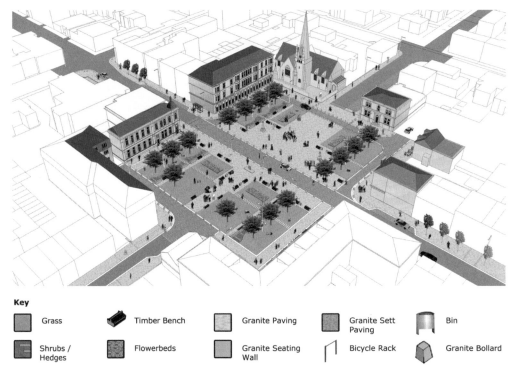

Key

Grass	Timber Bench	Granite Paving	Granite Sett Paving	Bin
Shrubs / Hedges	Flowerbeds	Granite Seating Wall	Bicycle Rack	Granite Bollard

4.4.2 The reorganisation of Colquhoun Square included rerouting traffic, reorganising parking and creating a range of spaces for civic use

ACTIVITIES AND EVENTS

Creating a range of different opportunities for people to use the square increases the inclusivity of the space and allows it to accommodate everyday uses – sitting, meeting, chance encounters and café culture – as well as more significant community events and festivals (see Figure 4.4.3). The town has held successful large-scale events within Colquhoun Square: a fireworks and autumn festival, winter festival with ice rink, several farmers markets, and charity events. These events encourage and attract more people into the town centre and support trade for local businesses, helping support a sustainable economy.

4.4.3 Colquhoun Square caters for a range of everyday activities and chance encounters

4.4.4 The outdoor museum threads through Colquhoun Square

AN 'OUTDOOR MUSEUM'

The redevelopment is supported by an arts strategy which draws on local history and heritage. Public engagement identified the desire for a new museum. The rich history of the town includes Charles Rennie Mackintosh, TV pioneer John Logie Baird and local figures such as Henry Bell who kick-started Helensburgh's development as a tourist resort and who introduced the first commercial steamship in Europe. In collaboration with local people, this has been captured in an 'outdoor museum' threaded through the new public space (see Figure 4.4.4). While acting as traffic control, bespoke bollards become plinths to permanently display local treasures, objects of significance and newly commissioned artworks. The first of these artworks include a series of historic artefacts encased in acrylic, bronze and stone reproductions of original objects and three specifically commissioned pieces by artists Lesley Carruthers, Kate Ives and Chris Coleman-Smith.

'It was just such a proud day for myself and my family to be part of what will be known as the first outdoor museum and to have a small part in the history of the town. I know I speak for all of my family when I say thank you for bringing our wee story to life.'

Elaine Crichton, local resident

CONNECTING BEYOND THE SQUARE

Beyond the square, the redevelopment created improved connections to the esplanade from the adjacent streets. Surrounding streets benefit from wider pavements with materials to match the square while the number of pedestrian access points to the beach and esplanade has been increased (*see* Figure 4.4.5). Public amenities – such as the esplanade toilet block – have been refurbished, the number of seats and benches has been increased and new informal play spaces have been added. Clear mapping, improved signage and space for community notices has removed unnecessary clutter from the streetscape. The improved quality of the public realm is reported to be benefitting the local economy with increased private sector investment and increased accessibility to the town centre.

4.4.5 The streetscape around Colquhoun Square has been refurbished and street clutter has been removed

---

'The project has seen a significant investment which will, I am sure, provide real, long-lasting and tangible benefits to local people and businesses. We are already seeing significant private sector investment in the town and are hoping to use this project as a springboard to further growth.'

Councillor Gary Mulvaney, 2016

CONCLUSION

The project has rejuvenated a major public square at the heart of the town, introducing a range of civic functions, planting and greens space. The design of the outdoor museum creatively integrates the display of the history and heritage of Helensburgh into the design of the square. A connected series of high-quality public spaces, including neighbouring streets and the esplanade, enhance the visitor experience and provide a high-quality setting for the historic town.

TRANSFORMATIONS

- **Connections:** a sensitive design response knits the town's public spaces together, encouraging a vibrant and active street life while respecting the historic town fabric.

- **Outdoor museum:** the outdoor museum reveals and enriches the story of the town, capturing local history and knowledge through a highly visible and continually growing installation that replaces standard street furniture.

- **An active asset:** as well as everyday activities, the space hosts events and festivals and has been a catalyst for further change and redevelopment.

- **Civic offer:** physical and economic regeneration have redefined and broadened the town centre offer, moving beyond retail and creating a civic heart to the life of the town.

CREDITS

Client: Argyll and Bute Council

Landscape architect / Urban Design / Community Consultation: Austin-Smith:Lord

Contractor: MacLay Civil Engineering Ltd

Engineers: O'Connor Sutton Cronin

Cost consultant: Robinson Low Francis

Traffic and transport: Transport Planning Ltd

Consultation and planning: Turley Associates

Consultation and public art: WAVE*particle*

Consultation and statement of participation: Turley Associates

CDM: Aecom

Awards: 2016 Scottish Design Award; 2016 RIAS Award; 2016 Saltire Society Arts in Public Places Award

4.5 CLONAKILTY 400, CLONAKILTY

Location: Clonakilty, West Cork, Ireland

Population: 4,592

Status: Completed 2017

Clonakilty 400 demonstrates the value of long-term stewardship in creating positive change. Since the 1960s County Cork has been unique in Ireland in having Town Architects with a civic role in working closely with communities to establish town development plans and to deal with planning applications. However, this role has diminished as priorities have changed. The success of Clonakilty 400 lies in the close collaboration between community and the local authority through the role of a civic architect, which has resulted in successful urban regeneration.

4.5.0 Main Street in Clonakilty during carnival

SITE AND CONTEXT

Clonakilty is a small seaside town west of Cork in the south of Ireland. Originally manufacturing cotton and linen, the town's growth is reflected in high-quality Georgian and Victorian architecture and a multitude of mills, warehouses and industrial buildings around the town. The closure of the railway in the 1960s led to a period of decline as it became isolated from Cork. However, its location close to the sea and beaches has made the town a centre for tourism and an attractive place to live, work and visit. Clonakilty has a broad range of community groups and, despite Ireland no longer having town councils, has retained a town mayor as a symbol of the community's desire to lead in considering the future of the town. Today, it has a strong sense of pride and local distinctiveness combined with a sense of entrepreneurism and openness to new ideas and concepts.[11]

To celebrate the 400th anniversary of the town's charter, the former town council initiated a heritage-led urban design plan – Clonakilty 400 – to reinvigorate the town's public spaces. The brief set out to re-establish social activities in the public realm and make residents aware of the value of its historic townscape. The focus was on providing new civic 'living rooms' for events and activities, replacing the dominance of the car with priority for people, renovating tired shop fronts and promoting re-occupation of empty buildings.[12]

ENGAGEMENT PROCESS

Working as 'community problem solver', the Town Architect was uniquely placed to be able to engage, generate and promote effective civic input as well as championing the town's built environment.[13] The role enables local character to be preserved and enhanced through quality design, public participation and promotion of visual awareness. The community was involved in decisions at all stages of the project, from building the project brief to decisions on the final design.

Initially, the Town Architect set out to empower local citizens by gathering local expertise, collaboratively building a brief which responded to local priorities. Local experts and community leaders engaging in the process became project champions, working with each other and the design team, to shape the direction of the project. Through extensive analysis, a vision for the town was developed that was supplemented by a new layer of design for inclusive public life, informed by experiences of successful sociable public spaces elsewhere in Europe. Roles within the team were identified for champions such as the town manager, chamber of commerce, heritage groups and politicians to ensure a broad representation in decision-making. The approach further aimed to inspire people to care by creating collaboration between local people through the sharing economy, connecting people and their stories to the place and allowing space for innovation and experimentation. The outcome of the process is a strong sense of ownership, increased civic stewardship and economic development.

PHASE 1

The first phase of the project focused on two main spaces, Asna Square and Emmet Square. Loss of parking on the high street was balanced by the opportunity to create safe, inclusive and green spaces for all ages and abilities, creating a sense of place and reducing the dominance of the car. New 'mini squares' at important locations improve the legibility of the townscape and invite people to linger in these outdoor rooms. These well-designed, shared spaces work hard in the narrow streets and demonstrate the potential of changing priority from vehicles to pedestrians in the historic environment.

At Asna Square, a geometric elliptical paving pattern creates a shared surface to accommodate passing cars, seating spilling out of cafés and a new pocket park (see Figure 4.5.1 and 4.5.2). With minimal road markings or signage, the design of the space gives pedestrians priority and creates a space for informal meetings and gatherings.

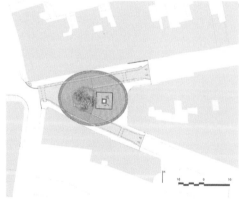

4.5.1 Asna Square, a shared surface around a mature tree

4.5.2 Plan of Asna Square

Emmet Square, a more formal square surrounded by two- and three-storey Georgian buildings has been re-landscaped (see Figure 4.5.3). A mix of grassed areas, planting, hard landscape and a new water feature and sculpture offer potential for a variety of uses for the space (see Figures 4.5.4 and 4.5.5). The rejuvenation of the square has encouraged the restoration of many of the Georgian buildings around the square and the renovation of Michael Collins House as a museum.

4.5.3 Emmet Square combines green space with planting, hard landscape and new fountains

4.5.4 Emmet Square includes a new water fountain

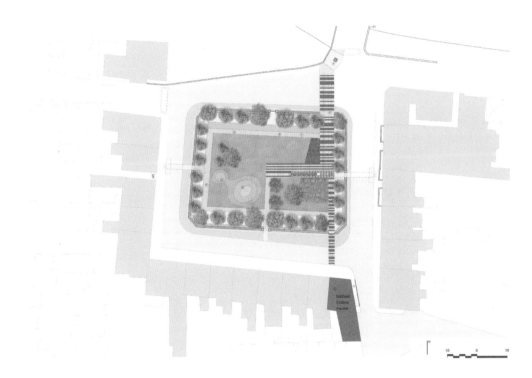

4.5.5 Plan of Emmet Square

PHASE 2

The second phase, focused on the main streetscape, arose from the need for a civil engineering scheme for new drainage which required extensive excavation along the main street. Rather than reinstating the existing hard landscapes, the Town Architect was able to adopt a holistic, design-led approach to reconsider the public realm and its potential for improvement. The need was identified for safe and accessible streets and the establishment of pedestrian priority. Raised traffic tables acting as shared space and high-quality materials continue the language established in Asna and Emmett Squares. Street clutter was reduced and road markings minimised, creating a cleaner and more legible streetscape. The raised traffic tables and pocket parks act as small-scale public spaces, encouraging informal gathering and inviting people to use the street. Street furniture and trees act to create enclosure and eliminate the need for bollards (see Figure 4.5.6). Irish Blue Limestone extends the language of the squares. Coloured recycled glass tiles reflect the colours of the streetscape; the colours were chosen with local shopkeepers who made suggestions to reflect their particular shop front. Surface features change where the paving meets the building line, making legible the transition from public to private zones.

'The town is an outstanding example of what the "Architect in the community" approach can achieve.'

Judges, Academy of Urbanism Great Town Award 2017[14]

4.5.6 High-quality street furniture sits on Irish Blue Limestone paving

CONCLUSION

The success of the project can be seen in physical terms through a reduced vacancy rate, new town patrons and increased investment. However, the real impact has been in the vibrancy and renewed sense of community evident in the town. From everyday meetings and greetings to town-wide events such as the International Guitar Festival, Old Costumes Fair or Street Carnival, the town centre has become a place for public life and conviviality. The redevelopment of the public realm was originally a civil engineering project requiring extensive excavation but joined-up thinking and smart use of public funding has resulted in a transformative project for the town. The same approach has been used for a Flood Relief Scheme currently under construction where collaboration between the engineers and the local authority through a holistic design approach have maximised public realm improvements and community outcomes.

TRANSFORMATIONS

- **The Town Architect in the community:** the Town Architect provides stewardship and encourages active participation, which has resulted in a strong sense of place and community ownership.

- **Holistic design:** the holistic design approach taken has delivered major streetscape improvements out of a civil engineering scheme. Collaboration with engineers and infrastructural funding across public bodies maximises public benefit of necessary improvements.

- **Connections:** a connected series of high-quality, friendly public spaces create different opportunities for people to gather socially.

- **Shared space:** careful consideration of shared space and removal of street clutter has shifted the balance from car to pedestrian. Use of pocket parks, well-placed and selected street furniture and raised traffic tables has created a safe and inclusive public realm.

CREDITS
Client: Cork County Council

Architect: Cork County Council Architects Department

Awards: RIAI Public Choice Award 2014 (Phase 1); Academy of Urbanism Great Town Award 2017; Best Place, RIAI Architecture Awards 2017; Gubbio Prize 2018

CORWEN

WREXHAM

CHAPTER 5

Long-term Strategies: Future Visions for Smaller Settlements

5.1 RECENT INITIATIVES TO SHAPE FUTURE PLACES

While the previous chapters have explored the potential of individual projects to positively transform their environment, this section examines the potential of architects to contribute to long-term visions alongside local people.

There have been a number of recent attempts to develop locally specific guidance and town plans. The Countryside Commission and Historic England developed Village Design Statements in the early 2000s. While written by local people, these documents were focused on the visual character of a place and often lacked a vision for the future of a village. In contrast, the Market Towns Initiative (MTI) aimed to realise regeneration projects through a strategic action planning process addressing socio-economic and environmental challenges. 140 pilot towns were selected, based on their potential to act as a service centre and a focus for growth.[1] While some towns benefitted from the programme, many found the approach difficult to navigate and the paperwork complex. Difficulties bridging from policy to implementation was further complicated by a lack of personnel and resources at some regional agencies.[2]

Perhaps the most successful partnership to emerge from the MTI was Yorkshire Forward's Renaissance Market Towns programme (RMT). Launched in 2003, the 10-year programme aspired to deliver sustainable communities through ambitious but achievable 25-year targets. Through collaboration between formal town teams and regional practices, a wide range of physical, social and economic regeneration projects were realised. While these projects have been successful, they have been implemented by national and regional government rather than being place-specific and locally driven. This 'guiding hand', with the ability to provide funding for both developing a plan and delivering projects, has ensured success. With resources now at a premium and the government implementing increasingly stringent budgetary restrictions, these funding driven approaches are becoming more difficult for local authorities to justify. Furthermore, government-initiated programmes are often short-lived and transitory, whereas small places require sustained, long-term and place-sensitive processes.[3] The pressure to 'hit the ground running'[4] has often meant little time to fully form strategic thinking and limited or ineffectual engagement with local communities.[5]

LOCALISM AND COMMUNITY-LED PLANNING

Evidence suggests solutions that are designed, developed and delivered locally are often better placed than central initiatives to understand local conditions and needs.[6] In England, Neighbourhood Planning, a core principle of the Localism Bill, offers communities increased power to shape their environment by developing their own local plans. Localism presents a unique opportunity to redistribute decision-making power to generate locally-led future visions, tailored to the needs of their environment. The National Planning Policy Framework aims to improve the quality of the landscape and built environment by encouraging designers to take account of character and distinctiveness while warning that planning policies should to be open to different approaches to development, neither fettering innovation nor imposing forms or architectural styles. However, experience suggests there are shortcomings in neighbourhood plans; they require large amounts of volunteer time and effort with relatively little support from professionals and often fail to produce locally distinctive development.[7]

In Wales, the Planning Act (Wales) 2015 and the Well-being of Future Generations (Wales) Act 2015 commit local authorities to improving social, economic, cultural and environmental well-being through participatory processes and public engagement. Alongside these top-down strategies, there is an emerging approach to increase engagement of local people in the plan-making process through the development of Place Plans authored by local people. While in England grants are available to communities engaged in neighbourhood planning, in Wales there is limited funding for professional support. This leaves voluntary organisations to take up the slack and requires local people to be active in undertaking analysis, funding applications and strategic thinking – skills that may be beyond many communities.

The Scottish government has promoted participatory planning through the Charette Mainstreaming Programme to generate community involvement in considering the future of towns and villages. Introduced to Scotland in 2011 from the USA, the charette brings together the public, stakeholders and designers over a four- to seven-day period in facilitated collaborative workshops and events. The outcome is a charette report with a masterplan or local strategy. The programme has been highly successful with over 48 places receiving funding for the process. Short-term intensive input is often highly beneficial to the communities in developing a vision and raising aspirations. However, follow-on funding is not always certain and requires communities to take charge after the event, making their role in long-term regeneration strategies uncertain. More recently, the charette programme has been replaced by the Investing in Communities Fund which, while still including the charette process, offers a broader range of approaches to community-led planning dependent on scope and scale.

While there is not a one-size-fits-all approach, these programmes offer an opportunity for local people to 'reclaim the initiative' and for the people who know their places best to influence its future. Localised projects provide opportunity for real community ownership and can result in schemes that make better use of local knowledge, assets and infrastructure.[8] Importantly, the increasing role of community-led initiatives has consequences for how we as designers conceive the urban environment and our role in enabling successful long-term visions and plans.

THE 'TOWN ARCHITECT'?

Architects and designers can have a key role in this process, acting as mediator, provocateur, initiator and consultant and offering routes to wider participation and successful implementation.[9] David Rock's 1999 RIBA presidential initiative, the Town Champion, identified the need for an independent expert who can understand the built environment, urban design, planning and property development.[10] Perhaps a similar role is needed today to support local communities facing change and provide long-term stewardship, working alongside a local authority to bring an independent voice that argues for place and people in the development and planning process. Working through an evidence-based, place-specific approach, a Town Champion would have the task of questioning assumptions and acting as a mediator between people, place and policy, providing an objective, impartial voice in what can at times be places fraught with conflicts of interest and passionate rival factions. The example of Public Practice – a social enterprise aiming to place architects and designers in the public sector to improve the quality of the built environment – is perhaps a contemporary example of this. Additionally, architects and designers can help to promote active citizenship, entrepreneurship and capacity building to achieve change,[11] contributing problem-solving skills and creativity to long-term planning and building long-term value for local communities.

COLLABORATING FOR CHANGE

There is the opportunity for close collaboration between professionals and local people to consider the long-term future of their place. It is vital that an in-depth understanding of a place and extensive community engagement provides a foundation to inform a long-term future vision. Do-it-yourself interventions can be combined with larger transformational projects to create long-term change. Smaller, more easily achievable stepping stones can create visible outcomes quickly, building community support. While for some places managing growth is the challenge, in others it may be sustaining or rethinking the purpose of a place. The following projects demonstrate the value of robust, evidence-based visions and strategies, supported by engagement with a wider section of stakeholders and the community, in creating long-term visions for towns and smaller communities. There is also significant potential for visions to be developed across multiple settlements, enabling a shift from competition between neighboring places to collaboration and interdependence. Long-term and generational commitment is needed, addressing challenges today but also looking to the future. Design is a powerful tool in this setting; architects and designers are ideally placed to lead, mediating between competing viewpoints and imagining innovative futures for smaller communities, founded on evidence, creativity and engagement.

Location: Ruthin, north Wales, UK

Population: 5,412

Status: Ongoing

Ruthin Future is a long-term community-led project to explore the future of a north Wales market town. Initiated by the town council in reaction to a feeling of increased powerlessness in the decision-making processes in their town, the project aimed to explore an alternative approach to regeneration that was 'bottom-up' rather than 'top-down'.

5.2.0 The refurbished St Peter's Square during the Ruthin Festival

SITE AND CONTEXT

Ruthin is a rural market town in Denbighshire, north Wales, located south of the urbanised north Wales coast and the A55 main trunk route from northern England to Snowdonia and Anglesey. With its medieval heart of castle, church and market place set on a hilltop in the Clwydian Range, the town falls away towards later suburban development around the historic core. A ring road to the north of the town and peripheral retail stores have distorted the town's centre of gravity and affected town centre businesses. The town boasts an internationally renowned and award-winning Craft Centre designed by Sergison Bates Architects, completed in 2008. The centre's changing exhibitions and studios attract tourists to the town and is popular with local people. However, its detached location on the ring road to the south makes attracting visitors to the historic town centre a challenge.

Ruthin Town Council commissioned the 'Ruthin Market Town of the Future Project' as a result of frustrations with their role in town-planning decision-making processes. A lack of joined-up thinking or long-term planning, combined with a reactive rather than proactive approach to development, led to numerous developments opposed by the town council being realised. Without a town plan or evidence base against which to assess incoming proposals, the town council had limited power to resist development or propose alternatives.

In 2009 Design Research Unit Wales (DRUw), an architectural studio based at the Welsh School of Architecture, Cardiff University, was approached by Ruthin Town Council to study the town and facilitate extensive public engagement to inform a community-led town plan. Working alongside the local community and town council, the practice sought to develop a method of working that would reveal the unique sense of place of this rural town before using this evidence to re-evaluate its potential. The project placed emphasis on an in-depth understanding of the built environment and public realm and aimed to develop a transferrable process of working and engagement that could be applied to other towns as well as for the benefit of the people of Ruthin.

ENGAGEMENT PROCESS: PHASE 1
Engagement with the town took place over two years of fieldwork visits, public consultations, exhibitions and events. The project commenced with a period of mapping and evidence building to understand the town's strengths and weaknesses (see Figure 5.2.1).

The finale of the engagement process was Ruthin Future, a week of activities involving practitioners, politicians, the local authority, local artists and makers, hoteliers, tourists, regeneration specialists, councillors, local school pupils and residents. The week combined traditional consultation techniques – such as an exhibition at Ruthin Craft Centre and a debate and conference hosted by Design Commission for Wales – with alternative engagement events – such as a photo-marathon photography competition, schools workshops and an artist-led drawing day – each exploring specific themes emerging from the engagement process (see Figure 5.2.2). With wide media coverage, the week-long intensive consultation period increased the profile of the project and reached a wider audience than would have been possible with one-off events.

5.2.1 Mapping of the historic burgage plots and hierarchy of routes around Ruthin

5.2.2 Collage of the engagement process carried out in the Ruthin Future process

A broad range of ideas and discussion were generated from the engagement events, but three overarching themes (*see* Figures 5.2.3 and 5.2.4) were identified:

1. The need to create a public heart for Ruthin focused on use by people rather than vehicles.

2. The need for safe connections between the historic town centre and the periphery for pedestrians and cyclists.

3. The importance of improving the tourist offer and town branding.

5.2.3 An aerial view of the town in 2022 showing the culmination of the vision

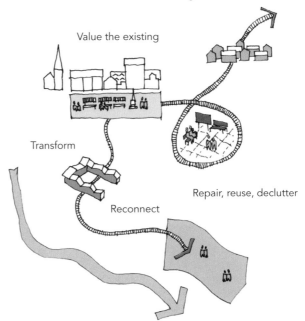

5.2.4 Value, transform, reconnect, repair – the core concepts behind the vision

The resulting town plan identified a series of small-scale affordable interventions to create maximum impact from minimum means. These were designed to be implemented incrementally as and when funding became available in a four-tiered approach that increases in scale, cost and complexity:

1. Making the most of the existing assets by celebrating and growing their potential.

2. Repairing, reusing and decluttering public spaces.

3. Reconnecting the historic town to the surrounding suburbs.

4. More significant transformational projects addressing key spaces.

The plan incorporated ongoing projects in the town as 'quick wins' to galvanise support for the plan. These included a proposal for an Arts Trail to link the Craft Centre to St Peter's Square (see Figure

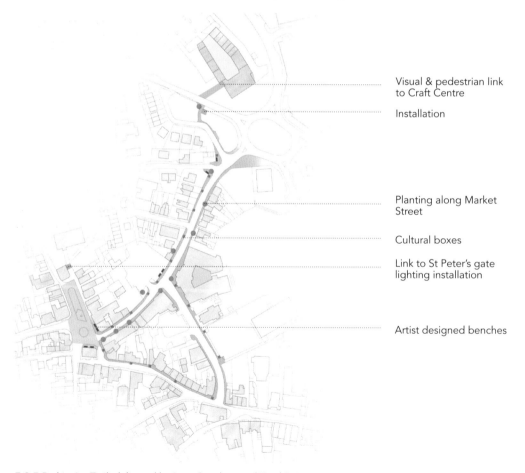

Visual & pedestrian link to Craft Centre

Installation

Planting along Market Street

Cultural boxes

Link to St Peter's gate lighting installation

Artist designed benches

5.2.5 Ruthin Art Trail, delivered by Lucy Strachan and Fred Baier, aims to draw visitors to the craft centre at the heart of the town

5.2.5), a key part of the strategy to draw visitors into the town centre, and a number of pedestrian access improvements as part of a 'Safer Routes to Schools' campaign.

ENGAGEMENT PROCESS: PHASE 2

In 2018 Ruthin Town Council commissioned a follow-up to the 2012 town plan to review the progress of the plan and update it with reference to the changing policy landscape in Wales and projects undertaken and delivered in the town since. In particular, the consolidation of services to reduce the local authority property portfolio, vacancy of a number of key buildings, relocation of the primary school to the outskirts and the potential for new housing development in the town centre were key areas for focus.

A mapping study gathered evidence about changes in the town and local residents were involved through a second Ruthin Future Week. Priority areas shifted to match the ambitions of the town. The need to rejuvenate the town square remained important but the consolidation of assets offered the opportunity to create new public uses for residents and tourists in the heart of the town, drawing people back in to the town centre. New linking threads connecting green spaces – parks, green space and riverside land – aim to create safe active travel routes around the town, particularly to the new school located on the periphery. Potential new housing sites were identified with the aim of creating a compact, walkable town but also to create homes for first-time buyers and the elderly to encourage all ages to live well in the town centre (*see* Figure 5.2.6).

'Since its inception in 2010, the Ruthin Future initiative has played an increasingly important role in the strategic development of Ruthin Town Council's projects and ambitions. Whilst we don't have the resources or administrative capacity to deliver all projects at the same time, each incremental improvement builds into the plan and brings added value to other connected initiatives. The plan is now updated annually through a week of public engagement events, where project updates are provided, new ideas sourced and additional areas for study developed.'

Gavin Harris, Ruthin Town Councillor, 2020

CONCLUSION

The Ruthin Future process has been undertaken over a nearly 10-year period, a time which has seen dramatic shifts in policy and funding for small settlements. Close collaboration has allowed the town council to take the lead in imagining the future of its

1 Create a heart to Ruthin
2 Connect green spaces
3 Safe routes to school
4 Living in the town centre
Green spaces
Strategic development sites
.... 10 minute walk from centre
- - - Riverside park

5.2.6 Ruthin Future 2 town plan

town, founded on evidence-based analysis and in collaboration with local people. Joining-up ideas and projects already within the community, such as a town tidy team, refurbishment and replacement of street furniture and the Arts Trail, set the foundations for a larger framework of transformational projects. Having a community-led plan with identified priorities has enabled the town council to apply for funding for major works to the public realm in St Peter's Square and win funding to take over and refurbish the Old Court House as a community hub thorough a community asset transfer. Most recently the framework set in the town plan was instrumental in the town's successful bid as the home of the North Wales Velodrome, bringing new investment to the town and broadening the town's visitor offer.

TRANSFORMATIONS

- **Building evidence:** the town plan was founded on an evidence-based approach that valued the sense of place, using gathered evidence and community engagement to shape a future vision.

- **Long-term engagement:** while initially a short-term commission, the project's extended two-year gestation enabled the town plan to respond to changes and challenges within the town in a way that a short-term vision could not.

- **Quick wins:** incorporating existing and emerging projects was beneficial in making visible the first incremental steps early into the plan's lifecycle and allowing the plan to be seen to 'hit the ground running'. Achieving local 'buy-in' and support through 'small wins' in this way can encourage the gradual tackling of larger issues.

- **Stewardship:** a long-term relationship between the town council and architect demonstrates the value of a sustained stewardship of place in realising an incremental vision.

CREDITS
Architects: Design Research Unit Wales / Coombs Jones architects+makers

Client: Ruthin Town Council

Funders: Ruthin Town Council, Beacon for Wales, Denbighshire County Council

Awards: Action for Market Towns Regional Award 2012, Partnership and Strategic Working Category

5.3 VILLAGE DESIGN GUIDES, SOUTH CAMBRIDGESHIRE

Locations: Caldecote, Fulbourn, Gamlingay, Histon and Impington, Over, Papworth Everard, Sawston and Swavesey, South Cambridgeshire, UK

Populations: Caldecote (1,737), Fulbourn (4,673), Gamlingay (4,900), Histon and Impington (11,280), Over (2,862), Papworth Everard (2,880), Sawston (7,145) and Swavesey (2,480)

Status: Completed 2019

Rural communities in high-demand areas are under considerable pressure for housing expansion. However, many communities are confronted with market-led growth which does not respond to existing patterns of development and can be unpopular with residents. Eight pilot studies in South Cambridgeshire show how co-creating design principles together with local people can help support and structure sustainable village growth. While each community has different challenges, the studies demonstrate the value architects and designers can bring to sensitive rural places in setting the ground rules for the next stage in their evolution.

SITE AND CONTEXT
South Cambridgeshire is a district characterised by diverse and distinctive villages. Their location within a high-growth area poses challenges of maintaining and enhancing their character while enabling sustainable growth led by the communities themselves. The aim for the South Cambridgeshire Village Design Guides is to explore the distinctive character of eight competitively selected villages to inform guidelines for how this can be enhanced by new development. The process was explicitly framed as an initiative to support housing growth funded by Ministry of Housing, Communities and Local Government's Design Quality Fund to develop exemplar village design guidance that could inform approaches in other places. The District Council sought expertise from social enterprise Public Practice, a pioneering scheme brokering year-long placements for built environment professionals in public sector organisations. This expertise helped procure a design-led approach to design guidance founded on gathered evidence and local knowledge.

THE PROCESS
An open call was issued for communities and eight were selected: Caldecote, Fulbourn, Gamlingay, Histon and Impington, Over, Papworth Everard, Sawston and Swavesey. Each community

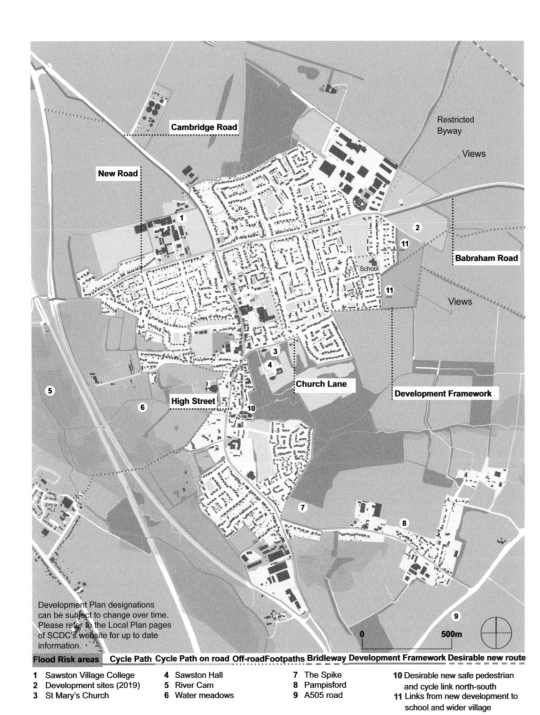

Cambridge Road

New Road

Restricted
Byway

Views

1

2

11

School

Babraham Road

11

Views

3

4

Church Lane

Development Framework

5

6

High Street

10

7

8

Development Plan designations
can be subject to change over time.
Please refer to the Local Plan pages
of SCDC's website for up to date
information.

9

0   500m

Flood Risk areas **Cycle Path** **Cycle Path on road** **Off-road** **Footpaths** **Bridleway** **Development Framework** **Desirable new route**

1 Sawston Village College	**4** Sawston Hall	**7** The Spike	**10** Desirable new safe pedestrian
2 Development sites (2019)	**5** River Cam	**8** Pampisford	and cycle link north-south
3 St Mary's Church	**6** Water meadows	**9** A505 road	**11** Links from new development to
			school and wider village

5.3.0 Aerial sketch of Sawston and its wider landscape area

was represented by a volunteer project champion supported
by a community steering group, including at least one parish
councillor and representatives from a broad range of interests
and backgrounds.

The pilot process aimed to develop a Village Design Statement for each village with the goal of adoption as Supplementary Planning Guidance giving them significant weight in the development and planning process. The expectation was for the statements to

- be concise, visually-led and forward-looking

- focus on the village community and represent the diversity of local views

- be design focused

- aspire to make new development appropriate, high quality and creative.

Four teams of consultants were appointed through an open selection process. The appointed practices work across boundaries and include masterplanning, urban design, architecture and community engagement as well as in policy and have expertise working in rural communities.

CREATIVE ENGAGEMENT WITH LOCAL PEOPLE

Each study began with evidence-gathering to establish the character of the villages, followed by workshops with the steering group and local people. The pilot studies followed a range of different approaches; the consultants shaped their engagement process to the individual community steering group's interests and their own perspective and expertise. Varying methodologies have been tested to assess what works well in teasing out the priorities and perceptions of local communities. Approaches included walking mapping workshops, participatory workshops with children, elderly residents and local societies, and joining community events and activities. In Papworth Everard and Caldecote, day-long workshops led to the production of village 'fanzines' (see Figures 5.3.1 and 5.3.2). This aimed to create a multi-voiced and diverse view of the community, created and edited by local people. The workshops and making of the fanzine stimulated a variety of valuable discussions which informed the identification of themes for the villages. These were presented back to local people to gain feedback and test their appropriateness.

These design-led processes creatively engaged local people in building evidence about their place to support design aspirations. What became evident from the process was that the communities are not anti-growth but are keen to be part of decision-making. From the consultation exercises, community priorities were identified that laid the foundation of the subsequent Design Guides. Housing growth and in particular the challenge of providing affordable housing was an important issue across the

5.3.1 Editorial meeting for the fanzine, Papworth Everard

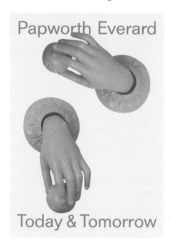

5.3.2 Cover of the fanzine,
Papworth Everard

villages. For example, in Sawston the desire for dense, sustainable development using varied and appropriate forms of housing emerged as a priority, particularly smaller-scale development on vacant plots close to the high street.

DESIGN GUIDANCE AND THEMES

In each village, analysis of the character of the place and the priorities identified by the communities informed the development of the Design Guides. This approach combined the expertise of the design teams in understanding the distinctive features of the village with the expert knowledge of local people who know their place best. For each village evidence-based guidance was developed to establish how new development could respond to, and integrate into, the existing built fabric. These guidelines build on the strengths of each village and promote integration of high-quality place-specific designs rather than pattern book development and suburban layouts.

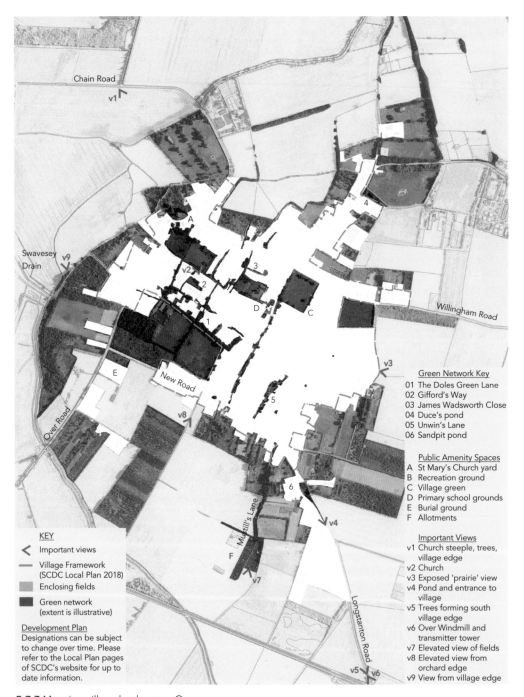

Green Network Key
01 The Doles Green Lane
02 Gifford's Way
03 James Wadsworth Close
04 Duce's pond
05 Unwin's Lane
06 Sandpit pond

Public Amenity Spaces
A St Mary's Church yard
B Recreation ground
C Village green
D Primary school grounds
E Burial ground
F Allotments

Important Views
v1 Church steeple, trees, village edge
v2 Church
v3 Exposed 'prairie' view
v4 Pond and entrance to village
v5 Trees forming south village edge
v6 Over Windmill and transmitter tower
v7 Elevated view of fields
v8 Elevated view from orchard edge
v9 View from village edge

KEY

‹ Important views

— Village Framework (SCDC Local Plan 2018)

◻ Enclosing fields

◼ Green network (extent is illustrative)

Development Plan
Designations can be subject to change over time. Please refer to the Local Plan pages of SCDC's website for up to date information.

5.3.3 Mapping village landscapes, Over

The priorities in Over highlighted the need to maintain and enhance the characteristic landscapes of enclosed fields, orchards, pastures and green lanes. The need to improve footpaths and add an increased provision of amenity space offered the opportunity to extend and enhance the distinctive village landscape (*see* Figures

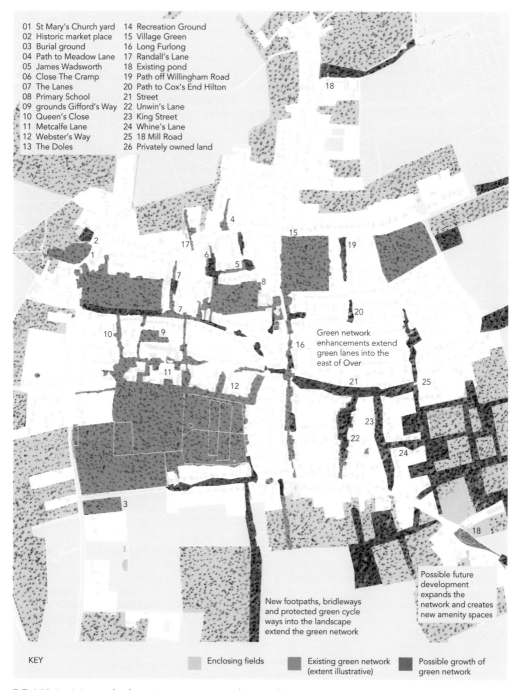

01 St Mary's Church yard
02 Historic market place
03 Burial ground
04 Path to Meadow Lane
05 James Wadsworth
06 Close The Cramp
07 The Lanes
08 Primary School
09 grounds Gifford's Way
10 Queen's Close
11 Metcalfe Lane
12 Webster's Way
13 The Doles
14 Recreation Ground
15 Village Green
16 Long Furlong
17 Randall's Lane
18 Existing pond
19 Path off Willingham Road
20 Path to Cox's End Hilton
21 Street
22 Unwin's Lane
23 King Street
24 Whine's Lane
25 18 Mill Road
26 Privately owned land

Green network
enhancements extend
green lanes into the
east of Over

New footpaths, bridleways
and protected green cycle
ways into the landscape
extend the green network

Possible future
development
expands the
network and creates
new amenity spaces

KEY

Enclosing fields

Existing green network
(extent illustrative)

Possible growth of
green network

5.3.4 Maintaining and enhancing a green network around Over

5.3.3 and 5.3.4). Green fingers connecting the village interior to
the landscape were identified as distinctive and opportunities
for extending and reinforcing the network of green spaces were
sought. This became a driving theme of the guidance, a means
to increase pedestrian connections at the village scale but also a

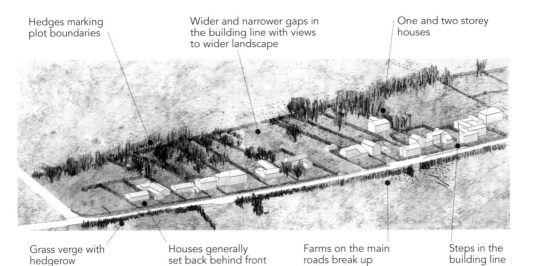

Hedges marking plot boundaries

Wider and narrower gaps in the building line with views to wider landscape

One and two storey houses

Grass verge with hedgerow

Houses generally set back behind front gardens

Farms on the main roads break up building line

Steps in the building line

5.3.5 The existing high street character, Swavesey

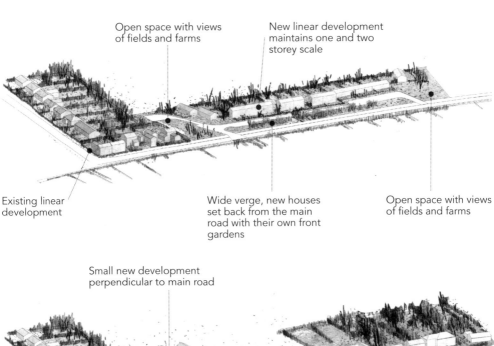

Open space with views of fields and farms

New linear development maintains one and two storey scale

Existing linear development

Wide verge, new houses set back from the main road with their own front gardens

Open space with views of fields and farms

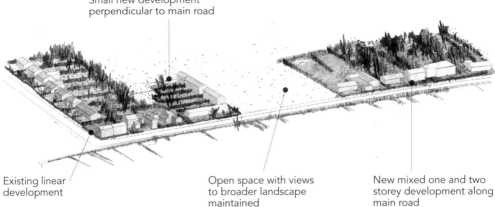

Small new development perpendicular to main road

Existing linear development

Open space with views to broader landscape maintained

New mixed one and two storey development along main road

5.3.6 Approaches to integrating new housing along the main road

principle at the heart of design guidance for new homes. Inclusion of informal green spaces between homes, green lanes and native hedgerows in new housing developments link them into the green network.

In Swavesey, the need for clear design strategies for new development along the main road was identified as a priority (see Figure 5.3.5). Along the existing main road, a distinctive character is created by hedges defining plot boundaries, views framed between houses to the wider landscape, patterns of setbacks from the road and front gardens along the street. The design guidance suggests new linear development should incorporate these distinctive elements (see Figure 5.3.6). Where infill takes place, gaps and views should be maintained, for example by setting the façade perpendicular to the road to maintain these views. Backland and infill development should be no higher or larger in scale than existing buildings to distinguish backland development from the linear pattern of the historic village.

ADOPTION PROCESS
In the process of development, the documents have been tested to ensure their viability. The draft guidance was used to inform pre-application discussions with developers and they have been reviewed by development management officers to assess their practicality in day-to-day use. In some of the villages, the Design Guides have been developed alongside emerging Neighbourhood Plans and have been particularly beneficial in giving communities a body of evidence to guide their long-term planning. The guides support Local Plan priorities by adding locally specific detail to what can be general strategic documents.

'The realisation that our village had traditionally developed lanes perpendicular to the High Street with terraced housing, thereby giving a distinctive characteristic, and that this would be a very appropriate way of developing affordable housing in new developments, was a real eureka moment for me.'

Village resident, Sawston[12]

CONCLUSION
Research by Public Practice suggests there is value for developers, local authorities and communities in developing specific and co-created design and landscape guidance for villages with capacity for growth.[13] It can ensure that local development benefits communities who feel their voice is being heard but also raises levels of knowledge and capacity for engagement with the planning system. The Village Design Guides demonstrate how

architects and designers can use their skills in understanding place and context alongside creative engagement techniques to deliver locally distinctive and place-specific guidance for rural places. The pilot projects are a test case for greater involvement of designers in the early stages of shaping village growth to ensure new development integrates with existing patterns while creating positive change focused on local needs. In working together, developers, planners and local communities can create developments that, rather than causing conflict, are welcomed by local communities and help villages to survive and thrive.

TRANSFORMATIONS

- **Professional expertise**: seeking expertise from Public Practice led to an effective procurement process leading to the co-creation of design-led, forward-looking design guidance.

- **Evidence-based, locally specific**: the Design Guides are founded in an in-depth knowledge of the villages, their character and distinctive features which inform the vision for future growth. While they share common characteristics, each plan identifies the key issues facing each village and focuses on means to create transformation in response.

- **Co-design**: working closely with local communities can build consensus around new development.

- **Integrating new development**: new proposals should consider how development is integrated into active travel networks, views and vistas, and the structure and fabric of the village.

CREDITS
Design teams: Citizens Design Bureau, DK_CM with Spacemakers and Europa, Emily Greeves Architects and Freddie Phillipson, Urban Silence

Client: South Cambridgeshire District Council

Public Practice associate: Hana Loftus

5.4 SHARING BOLSOVER

Location: Bolsover, Shirebrook, Clowne and South Normanton, Derbyshire, UK

Population: Bolsover (11,291), Shirebrook (9,760), Clowne (7,590) and South Normanton (9,445)

Status: Completed

Bolsover District has marked contrasts between areas of major investment and economic growth and the decline of traditional industries. Sharing Bolsover is guided by placemaking principles and the ideas of the people in the district combining transformative and fine-grained projects in a comprehensive vision for four communities.

5.4.0 Impression of Shirebrook Market Place

SITE AND CONTEXT
Located between Chesterfield, Sheffield and Nottingham, Bolsover District has four main towns and 19 villages, each with distinctive qualities and strong communities. The area has strong natural and historic assets; it is close to Sherwood Forest and the Peak District National Park and boasts historic attractions such as Hardwick

Hall, Bolsover Castle and Cresswell Crags. The area boomed during the Industrial Revolution due to its rich coal deposits. Today, the district faces a number of challenges. Proximity to the M1 motorway has attracted economic investment; however this is not evenly spread across the area and the repercussions of the loss of traditional industries, such as coal mining and textiles, are still keenly felt. While some areas are benefitting from investment, others are suffering from out-migration and lack of employment. Despite this, the area's population is predicted to grow with an additional 8,000 residents expected by 2030.[14]

ENGAGEMENT PROCESS
Architect Bauman Lyons has developed methodologies for successful community engagement through a series of projects over more than a decade. The project was a partnership between the council and the design team, where the council was fully engaged in stakeholder events and activities and provided additional support. An extensive engagement process engaged over 500 individuals, 377 community groups or parish/town councils (see Figure 5.4.1). Stakeholder workshops in each of the towns explored the challenges and strengths of the place and its surrounding communities, while chalkboard comments allowed people to give their feedback on the places they live.

THE VISION AND FRAMEWORK
The project looks towards 2033 and is guided by ideas and priorities gathered through engagement with the communities in the district. The ambition is to combine transformational and fine-grained projects to enhance the centres of the four main

5.4.1 Pubic engagement included chalkboard comments and workshops settlements and create better connections to outlying villages so these may also benefit from the improvements. The vision for each community was guided by three key principles:

1. **Building on what exists**: addressing weaknesses and barriers to prosperity and enhancing existing organisations, assets and initiatives.

2. **Embracing the future**: understanding how the changing nature of work, the shifting role of the high street, the impact of reducing carbon emissions and better connectivity can drive bold innovations in how people live. The projected growth following these trends have potential to improve the desirability and viability of the district's towns and villages.

3. **Co-producing regeneration**: the vision recognises that top-down strategies have failed to deliver sustainable regeneration and that many bottom-up strategies have been short-lived. A key principle is to encourage collaboration between councils and local communities through community based organisations such as community land trusts and community asset transfers.

The framework identifies three district-wide cross-cutting themes – connect, diversify and enhance. The district suffers from poor connections between the towns and villages; a major proposal in the framework is the development of a network of 'greenways' that improves connectivity and encourages active travel but also improves the quality of important environmental and visitor assets. This builds on existing projects and planned upgrades to the existing networks. The district is expected to grow, and strategic development sites have been identified by the council to accommodate housing and business growth. The framework proposes to create smaller housing developments on brownfield and infill sites as well as an infrastructure of co-working spaces, incubators and business support to encourage growth of business and social enterprise. Finally, investment in high-quality public spaces, improved shop fronts and a reduction in vehicle traffic will help support and grow independent retail, town-centre living and civic amenity.

These themes are supported by a framework of short-, medium- and long-term projects specific to each place (*see* Figures 5.4.2 and 5.4.3). These range from small-scale and easy to deliver to larger-scale, long-term projects. In total 20 key projects and 80 smaller 'stepping stones' have been identified across the district. These major projects address issues such as remodelling public space (*see* Figure 5.4.4), new pedestrian connections, proposals for important sites and identification of infill sites.

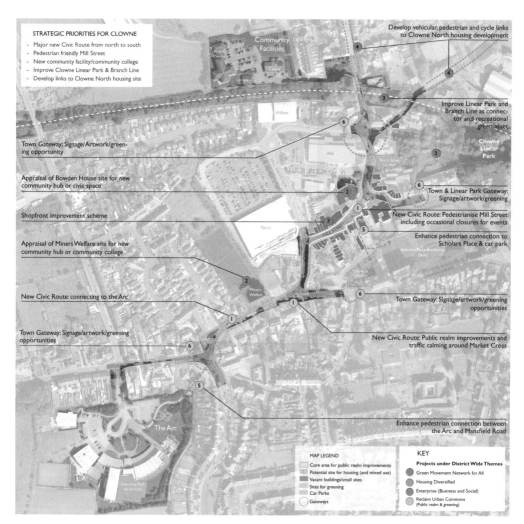

STRATEGIC PRIORITIES FOR CLOWNE

- Major new Civic Route from north to south
- Pedestrian friendly Mill Street
- New community facility/community college
- Improve Clowne Linear Park & Branch Line
- Develop links to Clowne North housing site

Develop vehicular, pedestrian and cycle links to Clowne North housing development

Community Facilities

Improve Linear Park and Branch Line as connector and recreational green asset

Town Gateway: Signage/Artwork/greening opportunity

Clowne Linear Park

Appraisal of Bowden House site for new community hub or civic space

Town & Linear Park Gateway: Signage/artwork/greening

Shopfront improvement scheme

New Civic Route: Pedestrianise Mill Street including occasional closures for events

Enhance pedestrian connection to Scholars Place & car park

Appraisal of Miners Welfare site for new community hub or community college

New Civic Route: connecting to the Arc

Town Gateway: Signage/artwork/greening opportunities

Town Gateway: Signage/artwork/greening opportunities

New Civic Route: Public realm improvements and traffic calming around Market Cross

The Arc

Enhance pedestrian connection between the Arc and Mansfield Road

MAP LEGEND
- Core area for public realm improvements
- Potential site for housing (and mixed use)
- Vacant buildings/small sites
- Sites for greening
- Car Parks
- Gateways

KEY

Projects under District Wide Themes
- Green Movement Network for All
- Housing Diversified
- Enterprise (Business and Social)
- Reclaim Urban Commons (Public realm & greening)

5.4.2 Strategic priorities for Clowne

For each individual project, a series of key actions are identified which help break down what could be daunting projects into achievable stages. Smaller stepping stone projects range in scale and include schemes such as establishing a town team, tidying and planting verges, improving gateways, creating temporary events and enhancing shop fronts. These do-it-yourself projects are in many cases achievable with limited investment. Coordinating small-scale projects within a coherent framework ensures that community groups and activities support the aims of the vision.

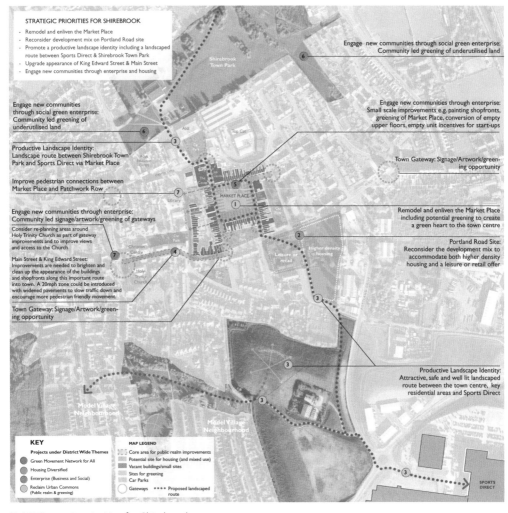

Engage new communities through social green enterprise: Community led greening of underutilised land

Engage new communities through social green enterprise: Community led greening of underutilised land

Engage new communities through enterprise: Small scale improvements e.g. painting shopfronts, greening of Market Place, conversion of empty upper floors, empty unit incentives for start-ups

Productive Landscape Identity: Landscape route between Shirebrook Town Park and Sports Direct via Market Place

Town Gateway: Signage/Artwork/greening opportunity

Improve pedestrian connections between Market Place and Patchwork Row

Remodel and enliven the Market Place including potential greening to create a green heart to the town centre

Engage new communities through enterprise: Community led signage/artwork/greening of gateways

Portland Road Site: Reconsider the development mix to accommodate both higher density housing and a leisure or retail offer

Consider re-planning areas around Holy Trinity Church as part of gateway improvements and to improve views and access to the Church

Main Street & King Edward Street: Improvements are needed to brighten and clean up the appearance of the buildings and shopfronts along this important route into town. A 20mph zone could be introduced with widened pavements to slow traffic down and encourage more pedestrian friendly movement.

Town Gateway: Signage/Artwork/greening opportunity

Productive Landscape Identity: Attractive, safe and well lit landscaped route between the town centre, key residential areas and Sports Direct

KEY

Projects under District Wide Themes
- Green Movement Network for All
- Housing Diversified
- Enterprise (Business and Social)
- Reclaim Urban Commons (Public realm & greening)

MAP LEGEND
- Core area for public realm improvements
- Potential site for housing (and mixed use)
- Vacant buildings/small sites
- Sites for greening
- Car Parks
- Gateways
- Proposed landscaped route

5.4.3 Strategic priorities for Shirebrook

5.4.4 Impression of South Normanton public realm improvements

CONCLUSION

Through three themes of building on what we have, embracing the future and co-producing regeneration, flexible visions founded on community collaboration have been established to transform the future of the district as a vibrant local economy with a strong sense of civic pride. Focusing on regrowth as a theme, pruning redundant town fabric and preparing the ground for change has resulted in forward-thinking frameworks that propose realistic and realisable projects.[15] Including 'quick wins' deliverable through a range of funding mechanisms helps build confidence in the frameworks and ensures they are live documents that inform ongoing development in the district. The frameworks have set the groundwork to enable the council to make larger bids for major town centre, infrastructure and housing projects, creating long-term change and raising the aspirations of local people.

TRANSFORMATIONS

- **Local knowledge**: the frameworks are rooted in local tacit knowledge and a place-specific understanding of the needs, qualities and opportunities of each town and village.

- **Action points**: breaking down large projects into easily digestible steps and stages make transformational projects manageable.

- **Stepping stones**: small-scale projects requiring limited investment offer the opportunity for a visible outcome of the framework to emerge quickly, led by local people.

CREDITS

Client: Bolsover District Council

Architect: Bauman Lyons Architects

Landscape architect: Camlin Lonsdale

Real estate advisor: GVA

Regeneration consultant: Accend

Arts and Heritage consultant: Deane Associates

Transport consultant: JMP

Awards: Finalist, National Urban Design Awards 2018

5.5 URBAN ACUPUNCTURE, SELB

Location: Selb, Bavaria, Germany

Population: 16,298

Status: Completed 2016

Post-industrial towns often suffer from low employment prospects leading to youth out-migration to places with more opportunities. In Selb, a series of linked projects demonstrate how working through small insertions in the urban fabric towards 'prevention rather than the cure' can stem this tide and sustain a shrinking town in the long term.

5.5.0 Haus der Tagesmütter, the Childminder's Centre, in its context

SITE AND CONTEXT

Selb is a town located in Bavaria, Germany, close to the Czech border. The town was founded in 1281 and flourished during the late industrial period following the establishment of the Rosenthal porcelain factory in 1879. During the 1990s the ceramic industry waned, leading to large-scale unemployment and a resulting decline in population, particularly amongst the young. Selb became a shrinking town.

To generate ideas for how to address the reducing, ageing population, the town was entered as a candidate site for the Europan 9 international competition. Taking an area of the inner town, the brief called for inventive ideas accommodate this changing demographic. The winning entry by Gutiérrez-delaFuente and TallerDE2 proposed a 'healing acupuncture' consisting of new housing, activities and infrastructure (see Figure 5.5.1). Intervention was organised in three stages:

1. The renovation and extension of existing dwellings.

2. The creation of new urban fabric.

3. An addition of new public programmes to redefine social spaces.

Following the competition win and after meetings with local stakeholders, it was decided to reorient the urban strategy from catering for an ageing population towards retaining and

5.5.1 Competition model showing a healing acupuncture consolidating the urban fabric through a series of 'stripes'

supporting the young. By keeping younger people in the town and attracting residents back to the town, it could be reinvigorated and its shrinking reversed. In response, the architects developed a number of projects: a child and infant day care centre, a football arena, a youth hostel and youth club, and experimental housing for young families.

THE PROJECT PROCESS

The building designs were developed within the framework of four main principles established in the competition entry.

1. At the urban scale, the perimeter of the existing urban blocks were strengthened to create strong street edges.

2. A network of public and semi-public spaces was established through these urban blocks, giving a sense of porosity and creating safe pedestrian routes.

3. New buildings were designed as a catalogue of 'stripes', responding to the urban context and seen initially as extensions of the existing homes but ultimately as zones of new housing and public facilities.

4. An open framework was designed to guide the process over time.

This action plan was founded on what the architects describe as a 'Preventative Urban Acupuncture' of small changes to the existing fabric to reactivate the centre of the town.

Within the action plan, a number of projects were developed: Haus der Tagesmütter (Childminder's Centre) for infants and children, Jugendzentrum and Jugendhotel (Youth Club, Hostel and Intergenerational Centre) for teenagers and young people, and IQ Innerstädtische Wohnquartiere (IQ Experimental Subsidised Housing) for young families.

The Childminder's Centre is a building self-managed by mothers' associations to care for children and infants during the working day and after school. It completes the last void in a varied urban façade, reinstating a street frontage. Located on a sloping site, it navigates the change in scale between a four-storey dwelling and a single-storey storage unit and opens the centre of the urban block to the town (see Figure 5.5.2). The stripes are expressed in different materials and visually express the programme of the building: management, greenhouse, storage, childcare spaces, and a passageway with a terrace above creating a connection into the urban block (see Figure 5.5.3).

5.5.2 The Childminder's Centre expresses its different functions through form and material finishes

5.5.3 A pedestrian route punches through the building into the open space behind

The youth club and hostel merge two building programmes that were previously isolated, encouraging new social connections between local users and visitors (*see* Figure 5.5.4). The new building fills voids in the existing urban fabric through nine stripes around a central yard. The youth club and hostel can be entered separately but located on a corner in a tightly knit part of the

5.5.4 The youth club and hostel

historic town, the building establishes a strong street edge through a varying two- to three-storey scale and asymmetric pitched roofs. The material of each stripe continues from façade to roof, creating a contemporary form differentiated from the historic fabric. The choice of colour responds to those found elsewhere in the town, such as the red shop front opposite, linking the building to its context.

The third project is apartments for young families, won in an invited competition as part of a Bavarian Government initiative to revitalise the centres of selected urban centres. The sloping site is located on the edge of the town centre close to the youth club and hostel. The IQ Project consists of 26 apartments, cellars, a parking garage and a biomass district heating system. The design proposal negotiates a level change between two parts of the town, taking advantage of the topography to embed the parking garage in a half-basement at the top of the site (*see* Figure 5.5.5). Six blocks of housing step across the site, connected by glazed loggias and open gardens. New pedestrian routes cut through the site, connecting two parts of the town which have long been isolated. A three-storey block to the north and a two-storey block with a monopitch roof create strong street edges and respond to the scale and history of their immediate surroundings. The simple building forms are carved to create balconies and entrances, revealing bold coloured linings within an otherwise understated material palette (*see* Figure 5.5.6). Apartments are designed with a spine of service areas, allowing the remainder of the space to be open plan, divided only by the recessed balconies.

CONCLUSION
A series of projects embedded in the town fabric aims to revitalise a shrinking town through measured and precise acupuncture. It sets out to introduce new uses and facilities that will appeal to the demographic that was migrating out of the town and make it a

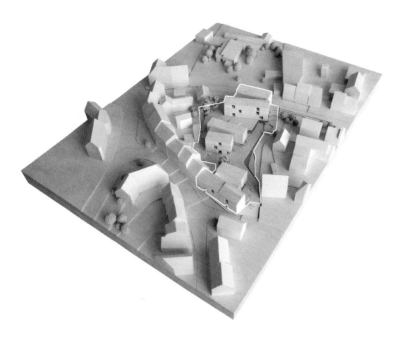

5.5.5 The IQ Project steps up a sloping site, connecting two areas of the town

5.5.6 A calm exterior is punctuated by brightly coloured reveals to balconies

desirable place to live for young people. The project demonstrates the value in a coordinated and long-term vision in tackling the place-specific issues faced by a particular place.

TRANSFORMATIONS

- **Urban acupuncture**: from an initial competition idea a number of projects have been developed that work within the existing town fabric through precise and measured interventions. These draw on the linear form of traditional plots and reinterpret these as a contemporary architectural language.

- **Prevention rather than cure**: rather than tackling the ageing population, the projects look to keep young people in the town by developing new facilities and homes, preventing migration.

- **Overlaying functions**: overlapping functions in the buildings aim to encourage people to mix and sets up chance encounters between different ages of people.

CREDITS
Client: Stadt Selb

Architects: Gutiérrez-delaFuente and TallerDE2

Local partner: SelbWERK GmbH, Helmut Resch

Collaborators: ZK for Europan 9 (competition phase)

Structure: Ingenieurbüro Schultheiß-Dietel

Installations: Ingenieurbüro Peter Möller, Ingenieurbüro IHP Versorgungstechnik

Lighting: Ingenieurbüro Netzel + Rennert

Fire Protection: Ingenieurbüro Eulitz

Construction: Karl Roth Baumeister GmbH & Co.KG

Surveyor: SelbWERK GmbH

Awards: 1st Prize Europan 9 Selb International Competition, Bauwelt Award 2013 'First Works'; Luis M. Mansilla COAM Award 2013; VII NAN Architecture Award 2013; Architektouren der ByAK 2014, Finalist XII BEAU Spanish Biennal 2013; Finalist IV Edition Arquia/Próxima Award 2014; Shortlisted FAD Awards 2014

CHAPTER 6

Conclusion

This book has set out to explore the positive role architects and designers can play in designing for change in small settlements. No two places are the same and different towns face different challenges. For some the issue is preventing stagnation, while for others growth and expansion bring different pressures of integrating new buildings and spaces. The case studies illustrate the value of a place-specific and evidence-led approach to the development of towns and smaller communities across the UK and a positive role for architects and designers to lead in that process. They reveal the potential for architects and designers to address certain challenges and contribute to the creation of thriving smaller settlements.

DEVELOPING PLACE-SPECIFIC APPROACHES
The projects demonstrate the possibilities of working in historic fabrics, creatively engaging local people, reconnecting town centres to their surroundings and integrating a mix of uses into town centres. Valuing the existing context and developing projects as a continuation and evolution of what already exists allows new architecture to become part of the evolving story of its place. A fine-grained approach leads to different responses to different places facing different challenges. While often referring to the scale, form and traditions of building, the projects suggest alternatives to existing situations; while not suggesting a break from the past, the projects remain open to the future and suggest new opportunities from existing challenges.

LOCAL PEOPLE WANT THEIR PLACES TO THRIVE
Engaging with local people is vital in developing new places and visions. The people who live and work in small communities know their place best and know the challenges they face. Creative engagement techniques, such as the making and performance workshops seen in Callan or the fanzine produced in south Cambridgeshire, can enable practitioners to gather opinion and build an understanding of local challenges, ideas and opportunities. There is a wealth of knowledge and skills to be found in smaller communities, and local people, groups and organisations do incredible work for the places in which they live. To succeed with implementing plans and projects, communities need to work together to mobilise a range of skills and resources whereby local people become fundraisers, coordinators and advocates for their place, a process architects can enable and guide. Professional input is also valuable in widening conversation and participation, mediating between groups and creating aspirational future visions supported by local people.

TOWN CENTRES SHOULD BE COMPACT AND INTEGRATED
The changing fortunes of high streets and town centres offers an opportunity to reimagine the function and role of town centres

and high streets. People should have the opportunity to live, work, learn and play in their town centres; catering for a broad demographic who believe in their place and have a sense of belonging supports the vibrancy of civic life. Locating schools, medical centres, community facilities and tourist attractions in town centres can increase footfall to local businesses and reduce car use. Encouraging new housing on brownfield sites, backland plots allows people to live close to town and village centres. While not applicable everywhere, resistance to the easy path of peripheral development and an appreciation of the importance of compact, well-connected places in creating thriving communities is vital in ensuring the long-term success of our small communities. There are examples of high-quality developments that break the formulaic model, but clients willing to challenge the norm and engage in alternative approaches remain few and far between. By championing town centres and exploring their opportunities, architects and designers can create distinctive new buildings, spaces and neighbourhoods that build on existing strengths and transform their futures.

HIGH-QUALITY, WELL-CONNECTED PUBLIC SPACES ARE VITAL

Public spaces, streets, lane, yards, and parks are important in people's perception of a place and in encouraging a convivial social life. In many places there needs to be a more equal balance between vehicle and pedestrian; the demands of the car should not dominate. The enclosed yards at Hebden Bridge Town Hall or the series of linked spaces in Clonakilty or Helensburgh show the value of a well-connected public realm that suggests how it could be used but is flexible enough to welcome a range of informal uses and occasional events. Accommodating a vibrant mix of possible uses – for example markets, seasonal events, play and informal, chance encounter, alongside trade and exchange – is essential. Different people need to be able use spaces at different times of the day and night in a cycle of activity and inhabitation, experiencing the theatre of everyday life and creating a sense of belonging.

ENSURING LONG-TERM CONTINUITY

The short terms of political office and the resulting cutting and changing of councillors, policy, targets and regulations opens up the risk of place-specific plans being cast aside as personalities and priorities change. In order to be successful, the outcomes need to be championed by professionals and supported by local people over the long term. The ongoing impact of austerity and the reduced ability of the public sector to fund statutory services will continue to impact on the ability of smaller places to create change, while the as yet unknown impact of the UK's vote to leave the European Union is likely to have a lasting effect on the economy and the construction industry. To be successful, these visions need to look to 15 or 20 years into the future and consider not only what is happening now but also future opportunities or challenges. Creating low-cost project 'quick wins' can build optimism and momentum around a longer-term plan or vision.

ARCHITECTS AND DESIGNERS HAVE AN IMPORTANT ROLE IN TRANSFORMING TOWNS

This book has sought to bring to the fore the multitude of ways architects and designers can take a greater role in shaping thriving smaller communities across the UK and beyond. What emerges is a positive and exciting vision of the potential impact we can have across a range of scales, from community engagement to new spaces and buildings to long term plans. Design quality is vital and with our skills in problem-solving, collaborative working and design we are well placed to take a lead in considering change in our towns and villages. The case studies show the range of ways in which we can lead the debate and the potential of the profession to deliver positive change. There is, furthermore, a role for practitioners to lead in championing place and distinctiveness for local people in the long term. The case studies support this argument: the Town Architect in Clonakilty, the long-term engagement of the author in Ruthin Future and the role of the Public Practice associate in south Cambridgeshire illustrate this is possible and the successes that can be achieved. Working in the grey areas between planning, landscape, architecture, geography and history creates a place for the designer in determining sites, developing visions and expanding their role in planning and development processes. With skills in analysis, evidence-building, problem-solving and community engagement, the architect and designer can act as a mediator between people, place and policy, providing an objective, impartial voice in what can at times be places fraught with conflicts of interest and passionate rival factions.

Now is the time for architects to join and lead this conversation, champion our smaller settlements and deliver positive change for our small towns and villages.

REFERENCES

FOREWORD

1 Jeffrey Bolhuis et al, 'Free Market': *Free Market: the Irish National Pavilion at the 16th International Architecture Exhibition*, La Biennale di Venezia 2018, www. freemarket.ie, 2019 (accessed 10 February 2020).

CHAPTER 1

1 Paul Knox and Heike Meier, *Small Town Sustainability*, Basel, Boston and Berlin: Birkhauser, 2009, p. 23.

2 Centre for Towns, *Our Towns* www.centrefortowns.org/our-towns (accessed 3 February 2020).

3 Paul Hindle, *Medieval Town Plans*, Princes Risborough: Shire Books, 1990, p. 6.

4 Lewis Mumford, *The City in History: Its Origins, its Transformations, and its Prospects*, New York: Harcourt Brace & World, 1966, p. 157.

5 Op. cit. Knox and Meier, 2009.

6 Russell E. Chamberlin, *English Market Towns*, London: Artus Books, 1993, p. 8.

7 Neil Powe, Trevor Hart and Tim Shaw, *Market Towns: Roles, Challenges and Prospects*, London: Routledge, 2007, p. 157.

8 Paul Courtney and Andrew Errington, 'The Role of Small Towns in the Local Economy and Some Implications for Development Policy', *Local Economy* 15.4 (2001), pp. 280–301.

9 Op. cit. Powe, Hart and Shaw, 2007, p. 29.

10 Action for Market Towns, *Market Town Healthcheck Handbook*, Action for Market Towns, Bury St Edmunds, 2005, p. 2.

11 Op. cit. Knox and Meier, 2009.

12 Alun Howkins, *The Death of Rural England: A Social History of the Countryside since 1900*, London: Routledge, 2003.

13 Nick Gallent, Johan Andersson and Marco Bianconi, *Planning on the Edge: The Context for Planning at the Rural-Urban Fringe*, London: Routledge, 2006, p. 81.

14 Op. cit. Knox and Meier, 2009, p. 75.

15 Department for Communities and Local Government, *Localism Bill: Neighbourhood Plans and Community Right to Build. Impact Assessment*, Department for Communities and Local Government, London, 2011, p. 15.

16 English Heritage and CABE, 'Building in Context', English Heritage and CABE, London, 2001.

17 Ibid. p. 5.

18 Jan Kattein, 'Talking Shops: How to Keep the High Street Alive', *RIBA Journal*, www. ribaj.com/intelligence/ high-street-regeneration-jan-kattein-architects-london, 2 June 2017 (accessed 24 February 2020).

19 Josh Holder, 'High Street Crisis Deepens', *The Guardian*, 30 January 2019.

20 GENECON, *Understanding High Street Performance*, Department for Business, Innovation & Skills, London, 2011.

21 New Economics Foundation, 'Reimagining the High Street: Escape from Clone Town Britain', 2005, p. 3.

22 Op. cit. Gallent, Andersson and Bianconi, 2006, p. 81.

23 Allan M. Findlay et al, 'Mobility as a Driver of Change in Rural Britain: An Analysis of the Links between Migration, Commuting and Travel to Shop Patterns', *International Journal of Population Geography*, issue 7, 2001, pp. 1–15 (p. 13).

24 Op. cit. Gallent, Andersson and Bianconi, 2006, p. 124

25 Ibid. p. 150.

26 Jane Jacobs, *The Death and Life of Great American Cities*, Modern Library edn, New York: Modern Library, 2011.

27 Orla Murphy, *Town: Origins, Morphology and Future*, Westport: Orla Murphy, 2012, p. 53.

28 Neil Powe, Rhona Pringle and Trevor Hart, 'Matching the process to the challenge within small town regeneration', *Town Planning Review*, issue 86, 2015, p. 196.

29 For further detail about the Charette process, see Charles Campion, *20/20 Visions*, London: RIBA Publishing, 2018.

30 Jeffrey Bolhuis et al, 'Free Market': *Free Market: the Irish National Pavilion at the 16th International Architecture Exhibition*, La Biennale di Venezia 2018, www. freemarket.ie (accessed 15 January 2020).

CHAPTER 2

1 Wendy Wilson and Cassie Barton, *House of Commons Briefing Paper number 07671: Tackling the Under-supply of Housing in England*, House of Commons Library, London, 2018.

2 Matthew Taylor, *Living Working Countryside: The Taylor Review of Rural Economy and Affordable Housing*, Department for Communities and Local Government, London, 2008, p. 53.

3 Action with Communities in Rural England, *ACRE Position Paper: Rural Housing*, Action with Communities in Rural England, Cirencester, 2017.

4 Rose Grayston, 'The roots of the rural housing crisis', Shelter, blog.shelter.org. uk/2018/07/rural-housing-crisis, 2018 (accessed 2 February 2020).

5 RIBA and Centre for Towns, *A Home for the Ages: Planning for the Future with Age-friendly Design*, RIBA and Centre for Towns, London, 2019.

6 Jeremy Poteus, 'HAPPI 4, The Rural HAPPI Enquiry. Rural Housing for an Ageing Populations: Preserving Independence', APPG for Housing and Care for Older People, London, 2018.

7 Avi Friedman, *Planning Small and Medium Sized Towns: Designing and Retrofitting for Sustainability*, London: Routledge, 2014.

8 Neil Powe and Zan Gunn, 'Housing Development in Market Towns: Making A Success Of "Local Service Centres"?' *Town Planning Review*, volume 79, issue 1, 2008, pp. 125-48 (p. 143).

9 CPRE and HTA Design LLP, *Unlocking Potential: Best Practice for Brownfield Land Registers*, CPRE and HTA Design LLP, London, 2017.

10 RIBA, *Ten Characteristics of Places where People want to Live*, RIBA, London, 2018.

11 PTE, HTA, Proctor & Matthews and PRP Architects, 'Distinctively Local', PTE, HTA, Proctor & Matthews and PRP Architects, London, 2019, p. 7.

12 Ibid. p. 7.

13 Ibid. p. 21.

14 Office for National Statistics, 'Economies of Ale', *Office for National Statistics*, www.ons. gov.uk/businessindustryand trade/business/activitysizeand location/articles/economiesof alesmallpubscloseaschainsfoc usonbigbars/2018-11-26 (accessed 24 April 2019).

15 Institute for Public Policy Research, *Pubs and places: The social value of community pubs*, IPPR, London, 2012, p. 29

16 See www.essexdesignguide. co.uk/. The guide was reviewed and updated in 2005 and 2018.

17 Eleanor Young, 'Time and Place', *RIBA Journal*, volume 123, issue 7, July 2016, pp. 8-12.

18 Op. cit. RIBA and Centre for Towns, 2019, p. 12.

CHAPTER 3

1 RIBA, 'Help us reinvent the British High Street', *RIBA Journal*, 15 February 2019.

2 Josh Holder, 'High street crisis deepens: 1 in 12 shops closed in five years', *The Guardian*, 30 January 2019 www.theguardian.com/cities/ ng-interactive/2019/jan/30/ high-street-crisis-town- centres-lose-8-of-shops- in-five-years (accessed 29 September 2019).

3 Mary Portas, *The Portas Review: An Independent Review into the Future of our High Streets*, UK Government, London, 2011.

4 Andrew Simms, Petra Kjell and Ruth Potts, *Clone Town Britain: The survey results on the bland state of the nation*, New Economics Foundation, London, 2005.

5 Office for National Statistics, *Comparing 'Bricks and Mortar' store sales with online retail sales: August 2018*, Office for National Statistics, London, 2018.

6 Neil Wrigley and Dionysia Lambrini, *High Street Performance and Evolution*, Southampton: University of Southampton, 2014.

7 New Economics Foundation, *Ghost Town Britain*, New Economics Foundation, London, 2005, p. 2.

8 Lorna Booth and Jennifer Brown, 'Post Office Numbers', *House of Commons Library Briefing Paper* no. 2525, 9 August 2018.

9 Unknown, 'Over a third of bank branches closed in under five years, Which? Reveals', press.which.co.uk/ whichpressreleases/over- a-third-of-bank-branches- closed-in-under-five-years- which-reveals/ (accessed 29 September 2019).

10 Op. cit. Portas, 2011.

11 Bill Grimsey, *The Grimsey Review 2*, Bill Grimsey, London, 2018.

12 Sir John Timpson, *The High Street Report*, UK Government, London, 2019.

13 Malcolm Fraser, *National Review of Town Centres: External Advisory Group Report: Community and Enterprise in Scotland's Town Centres*, Scottish Government, Edinburgh, 2013.

14 National Assembly for Wales Enterprise and Business Committee, *Regeneration of Town Centres*, National Assembly for Wales, Cardiff, 2012.

15 Steve Millington, Nikos Ntounis, Cathy Parker, Simon Quinn, Gareth Roberts and Chloe Steadman, *High Street 2030: Achieving Change*, Institute of Place Management, Manchester, 2018.

16 Ministry of Housing Communities and Local Government, 'Future High Streets Fund: call for proposals', UK Government, London, 2019.

17 Scottish Government, 'Town Centre Fund', www.gov.scot/ policies/regeneration/town- centre-fund/ (accessed 30 September 2019).

18 Julian Dobson, *How to Save our Town Centres: A Radical Agenda for the Future of High Streets*, Bristol: Policy Press, 2015.

19 Josephine Smit, 'There's Life Beyond Shops for Struggling Town Centres', *RIBA Journal*, 20 March 2019, www.ribaj. com/products/futurebuild- 2019-finding-a-prosperous- use-for-british-town-centres- panel-debate> (accessed 8 February 2020).

CHAPTER 4

1 Rosie Webb, *Back to the Future for Town Squares*, Freemarket, Ireland, 2018 www.freemarket.ie/01_ news_2.php (accessed 15 January 2020).

2 Ibid.

3 Neil Powe, Trevor Hart and Tim Shaw, *Market Towns: Roles, Challenges and Prospects*, London: Routledge, 2007, p. 150.

4 Avi Friedman, *Planning Small and Medium Sized Towns: Designing and Retrofitting for Sustainability*, London: Routledge, 2014, p. 72.

5 Mayor of London, *Better Streets: Practical Steps*, Mayor of London, London, 2009, p. 6.

6 Orla Murphy, *Town: Origins, Morphology and Future*, Westport: Orla Murphy, 2010, p. 56.

7 CABE, *Streets of Shame: Summary of findings from 'Public Attitudes to Architecture and the Built Environment'*, CABE, London, 2002.

8 Julian Dobson, *Grey Places Need Green Spaces: The Case for Investing in our Nation's Natural Assets*, Birmingham: Groundwork, 2012, p. 1.

9 Gordon Cullen, *The Concise Townscape*, London: Architectural Press, 1971.

10 These organisations include Abhainn Rí Festival, Asylum Productions, Equinox Theatre Company, Fennelly's of Callan, Monkeyshine Theatre, Tony O'Malley Residency, Workhouse Union and Trasna Productions.

11 Michele Grant, *Clonakilty – Great Town Award Assessment Report*, Academy of Urbanism, 2017, www.academyofurbanism.org.uk/clonakilty/ (accessed 22 February 2020).

12 RIAI Urban Design Taskforce, *Creating Places for People: The RIAI Town and Village Toolkit*, www.riai.ie/uploads/files/general-files/RIAI_TownandVillageToolkit.pdf (accessed 24 February 2020).

13 Ibid (accessed 24 February 2020).

14 Op. cit. Grant, 2017.

CHAPTER 5

1 Alison Caffyn, 'Market town regeneration: Challenges for policy and implementation', *Local Economy*, volume 19, 2004, p. 8.

2 Ibid., p.22.

3 Neil Powe, Rhona Pringle and Trevor Hart, 'Matching the process to the challenge within small town regeneration', *Town Planning Review*, volume 86, issue 2, pp. 177–202 (p. 196).

4 Ibid, pp. 177-202.

5 Paul Lawless, 'Understanding the scale and nature of outcome change in area-regeneration programmes: evidence from the New Deal for Communities programme in England', *Environment and Planning C: Government and Policy*, Issue 29, pp. 520–32.

6 Laura Blunt and Michael Harris, *Mass Localism: A Way to Help Small Communities Solve Big Social Challenges. A Discussion Paper*, NESTA, London, 2010.

7 Hana Loftus, *Practice Note 002: Growing Villages: How should village growth be shaped in rural areas?* Public Practice, London, 2019, p. 3.

8 Matthew Jones and Amanda Spence, 'Planning for well-being: a critical perspective on embedding well-being in community-led planning processes', in *Designing for Health and Wellbeing: Home, City, Society*, eds Matthew Jones, Fidel Meraz and Louis Rice, Delaware and Malaga: Vernon Press, 2019.

9 Doina Petrescu, Constantin Petcou and Corelia Baibarac, 'Co-producing Commons-based Urban resilience: Lessons from R-Urban', *Building Research & Information*, vol. 44, issue 7, 2016, pp. 717-36.

10 Dan Bone, *Town Champions: The President's Initiative*, London and Oxford: RIBA and Alden Press, 1999, p. 9.

11 Lynda Herbert-Cheshire, L. & Vaughan Higgins, 'From risky to responsible: expert knowledge and the governing of community-led rural development', *Journal of Rural Studies*, vol. 20, issue 3, 2004, pp. 289–302.

12 Op. cit. Loftus, p. 10.

13 Op. cit. Loftus, p. 13.

14 Bauman Lyons, *Sharing Bolsover!*, Bolsover District Council, p. 13, www.bolsover.gov.uk/index.php/39-resident/regeneration (accessed 9 March 2020).

15 Urban Design Group, *National Urban Design Awards 2018*, Urban Design Group, London, 2018, p. 11.

BIBLIOGRAPHY

Action for Market Towns, *Market Town Healthcheck Handbook*, Action for Market Towns, Bury St Edmunds, 2005

Action with Communities in Rural England, *ACRE Position Paper: Rural Housing*, Action with Communities in Rural England, Cirencester, 2017 Bauman Lyons Architects, *Sharing Bolsover!*, Bolsover District Council, Bolsover, www.bolsover.gov.uk/index.php/39-resident/regeneration (accessed 9 March 2020)

Bianconi, M., and Tewdwr-Jones, M., 'The Form and Organisation of Urban Areas: Colin Buchanan and Traffic in Towns 50 Years on', The Town Planning Review, vol. 84/no. 3, (2013), pp. 313-336.

Bishop, C., The Bishop Review: The Future of Design in the Built Environment, Design Council, London, 2011

Blunt, L. and Harris, M., *Mass Localism: A Way to Help Small Communities Solve Big Social Challenges. A Discussion Paper*, NESTA, London, 2010

Bolhuis, J., Butler, J., Delaney, M., Kennedy, T., Lord, L. and Murphy, O., 'Free Market': *Free Market: the Irish National Pavilion at the 16th International Architecture Exhibition*, La Biennale di Venezia 2018, www.freemarket.ie, 2019 (accessed 15 January 2020)

Bone, D., *Town Champions: The President's Initiative*, RIBA and Alden Press, London and Oxford, 1999

Booth, L. and Brown, J., 'Post Office Numbers', *House of Commons Library Briefing Paper* no. 2525, 9 August 2018, House of Commons, London, 2018.

CABE, *Streets of Shame: Summary of findings from 'Public Attitudes to Architecture and the Built Environment'*, CABE, London, 2002

Caffyn, A., 'Market town regeneration: Challenges for policy and implementation', *Local Economy*, volume 19, 2004

Campion, C., *20/20 Visions*, RIBA Publishing, London, 2018

Carmona, M., *Housing Design Quality: Through Policy, Guidance and Review*, Taylor & Francis, London, 2001

Centre for Towns, 'Our Towns', *Centre for Towns* www.centrefortowns.org/our-towns (accessed 3 February 2020)

Chamberlin, R.E., *English Market Towns*, Artus Books, London, 1993

Commission for Rural Communities, *State of the Countryside 2020*, Countryside Agency, Wetherby, 2003

Conzen M.R.G., *Alnwick, Northumberland: A Study in Town-Plan Analysis*, George Philip & Son Ltd, London, 1960

Conzen M.R.G. and Conzen M.P., *Thinking about Urban Form: Papers on urban morphology, 1932–1998*, Peter Lang, 2004

Courtney P. and Errington, A., 'The Role of Small Towns in the Local Economy and Some Implications for Development Policy', *Local Economy* 15.4 (2001), pp. 280–301.

CPRE and HTA Design LLP, *Unlocking Potential: Best Practice for Brownfield Land Registers*, CPRE and HTA Design LLP, London, 2017

Cullen, G., *The Concise Townscape*, Architectural Press, London, 1971

Department for Communities and Local Government, *Localism Bill: Neighbourhood Plans and Community Right to Build. Impact Assessment*, Department for Communities and Local Government, London, 2011

Dobson, J., *How to Save our Town Centres: A Radical Agenda for the Future of High Streets*, Bristol: Policy Press, 2015

English Heritage and CABE, 'Building in context', English Heritage and CABE, London, 2001

Essex Design Guide, www.essexdesignguide.co.uk. The guide was reviewed and updated in 2005 and 2018

Findlay, A.M. et al, 'Mobility as a Driver of Change in Rural Britain: An Analysis of the Links between Migration, Commuting and Travel to Shop Patterns', *International Journal of Population Geography*, issue 7, 2001, pp. 1-15

Fort, T., *The Village News*, Simon & Schuster, London, 2017

Fraser, M., *National Review of Town Centres: External Advisory Group Report: Community and Enterprise in Scotland's Town Centres*, Scottish Government, Edinburgh, 2013

Friedman, A. *Planning Small and Medium Sized Towns: Designing and Retrofitting for Sustainability*, Routledge, London, 2014

Gallent, N., Andersson J. and Bianconi M., *Planning on the Edge: The Context for Planning at the Rural-Urban Fringe*, Routledge, London, 2006

Gehl J. and Birgitte S., *How to Study Public Life*, Island Press, Washington, 2013

GENECON & Partners, *Understanding High Street Performance*, Department for Business, Innovation & Skills, London, 2011

Grant, M., *Clonakilty – Great Town Award Assessment Report*, Academy of Urbanism, 2017, www.academyofurbanism.org.uk/clonakilty/ (accessed 22 February 2020).

Grayston, R., 'The roots of the rural housing crisis', *Shelter*, blog.shelter.org.uk/2018/07/rural-housing-crisis/ 2018 (accessed 2 February 2020)

Grimsey, B., *The Grimsey Review 2*, Bill Grimsey, London, 2018

Gunn, S., 'The Buchanan Report, Environment and the Problem of Traffic in 1960s Britain', *Twentieth Century British History*, vol. 22, issue 4, 2011

Herbert-Cheshire, L. and Higgins, V., 'From risky to responsible: expert knowledge and the governing of community-led rural development', *Journal of Rural Studies*, vol. 20, issue 3, 2004, pp. 289-302

Hindle, P., *Medieval Town Plans*, Shire Books, Princes Risborough, 1990

Holder, J., 'High street crisis deepens: 1 in 12 shops closed in five years', *The Guardian*, 30 January 2019 www.theguardian.com/cities/ng-interactive/2019/jan/30/high-street-crisis-town-centres-lose-8-of-shops-in-five-years (accessed 29 September 2019)

Howkins, A., *The Death of Rural England: A Social History of the Countryside since 1900*, Routledge, London, 2003

Institute for Public Policy Research, *Pubs and places: The social value of community pubs*, IPPR, London, 2012

Jacobs, J., *The Death and Life of Great American Cities*, Modern Library edn, Modern Library, New York, 2011

Jones, M. and Spence, A., 'Planning for well-being: a critical perspective on embedding well-being in community-led planning processes', in *Designing for Health and Wellbeing: Home, City, Society*, eds Matthew Jones, Fidel Meraz and Louis Rice, Vernon Press, Delaware and Malaga, 2019

Kattein, J., 'Talking Shops: How to Keep the High Street Alive', *RIBA Journal*, 2 June 2017 www.ribaj.com/intelligence/high-street-regeneration-jan-kattein-architects-london (accessed 24 February 2020)

Knox, P. and Meier H., *Small Town Sustainability*, Birkhauser, Basel, Boston and Berlin, 2009

Lawless, P., 'Understanding the scale and nature of outcome change in area-regeneration programmes: evidence from the New Deal for Communities programme in England', *Environment and Planning C:*

Government and Policy, Issue 29, pp. 520-32

Loftus, H., *Practice Note 002: Growing Villages: How should village growth be shaped in rural areas?* Public Practice, London, 2019

Lynch, K., *The image of the City*, MIT Press, Cambridge, Mass., 1960

Mayor of London, *Better Streets: Practical Steps*, Mayor of London, London, 2009

Millington, S., Ntounis, N., Parker, C., Quinn, S., Roberts, G. and Steadman, C., *High Street 2030: Achieving Change*, Institute of Place Management, Manchester, 2018

Ministry of Housing Communities and Local Government, 'Future High Street Fund: call for proposals', UK Government, London, 2019

Mumford, L., *The City in History: Its Origins, its Transformations, and its Prospects*, Harcourt Brace & World, New York, 1966

Murphy, O., *Town: Origins, Morphology and Future*, Orla Murphy, Westport, 2012

National Assembly for Wales Enterprise and Business Committee, *Regeneration of Town Centres*, National Assembly for Wales, Cardiff, 2012

New Economics Foundation, *Ghost Town Britain*, New Economics Foundation, London, 2005

New Economics Foundation, *Reimagining the High Street: Escape from Clone Town Britain*, June 2005

Office for National Statistics, *Comparing 'Bricks and Mortar' store sales with online retail sales: August 2018*, ONS, London, 2018

Office for National Statistics, 'Economies of Ale', *Office for National Statistics*, www.ons.gov.uk/businessindustryandtrade/business/activitysizeandlocation/articles/economiesofalesmallpubs

closeaschainsfocusonbigbars/2018-11-26 (accessed 24 April 2019)

Owen, S., 'The Town Observed: Looking at Settlements from the Surrounding Landscape,' in *Journal of Urban Design*, volume 14 issue 4, 2009, pp. 537-55

Petrescu, D., Petcou, C. and Baibarac, C., 'Co-producing Commons-based Urban resilience: Lessons from R-Urban', Building Research & Information, vol. 44, issue 7, 2016, pp. 717-36

Portas, M., *The Portas Review: An Independent Review into the Future of our High Streets*, UK Government, London, 2011

Poteus, J., 'HAPPI 4, The Rural HAPPI Enquiry. Rural Housing for an Ageing Populations: Preserving Independence', APPG for Housing and Care for Older People, London, 2018

Powe, N. and Gunn, Z., 'Housing Development in Market Towns: Making A Success Of "Local Service Centres"?' *Town Planning Review*, volume 79, issue 1, 2008, pp. 125-48

Powe, N. Hart, T. and Shaw, T., *Market Towns: Roles, Challenges and Prospects*, Routledge, London, 2007

Powe, N., Pringle, R. and Hart, T., 'Matching the process to the challenge within small town regeneration', *Town Planning Review*, issue 86, 2015, pp. 177–202

PTE, HTA, Proctor & Matthews and PRP Architects, 'Distinctively Local', PTE, HTA, Proctor & Matthews and PRP Architects, London, 2019

New Economics Foundation, *Ghost Town Britain*, New Economics Foundation, London, 2005

RIAI Urban Design Taskforce, *Creating Places for People: The RIAI Town and Village Toolkit*, www.riai.ie/uploads/files/general-files/RIAI_TownandVillageToolkit.pdf (accessed 24 February 2020)

RIBA, 'Help us reinvent the British High Street', *RIBA Journal*, 15 February 2019

RIBA, *Ten Characteristics of Places where People want to Live*, RIBA, London, 2019

RIBA and Centre for Towns, *A Home for the Ages: Planning for the Future with Age-friendly Design*, RIBA and Centre for Towns, London, 2019

RIBA Journal, 'Help us reinvent the British High Street', *RIBA Journal*, www.ribaj.com/products/future-town-centres-competition-2019-aco-technologies-high-streets-dover-tredegar-byker (accessed 29 September 2019)

Sacramento, N. and Zeiske, C., *ARTocracy. Art, Informal Space and Social Conscience: A curatorial Handbook in Collaborative Practice*, Jovis, Berlin, 2010

Scottish Government, 'Town Centre Fund', *Scottish Government*, www.gov.scot/policies/regeneration/town-centre-fund/ (accessed 30 September 2019)

Simms, A., Kjell, P. and Potts, R., *Clone Town Britain: The survey results on the bland state of the nation*, New Economics Foundation, London, 2005

Smit, J., 'There's Life Beyond Shops for Struggling Town Centres', *RIBA Journal*, 20 March 2019, www.ribaj.com/products/futurebuild-2019-finding-a-prosperous-use-for-british-town-centres-panel-debate> (accessed 8 February 2020)

Taylor, M., *Living Working Countryside: The Taylor Review of Rural Economy and Affordable Housing*, Department for Communities and Local Government, London, 2008

Timpson, J., *The High Street Report*, UK Government, London, 2019

Webb, R., *Back to the Future for Town Squares*, Freemarket, Ireland, 2018 www.freemarket.ie/01_news_2.php (accessed 15 January 2020)

Which?, 'Over a third of bank branches closed in under five years, Which? Reveals', *Which?* press.which.co.uk/whichpressreleases/over-a-third-of-bank-branches-closed-in-under-five-years-which-reveals/ (accessed 29 September 2019)

Wilson, W. and Barton, C., *House of Commons Briefing Paper number 07671: Tackling the Under-supply of Housing in England*, House of Commons Library, London, 2018

Wrigley, N. and Lambrini, D., *High Street Performance and Evolution*, University of Southampton, Southampton, 2014

Young, E., 'Time and Place', *RIBA Journal*, volume 123, issue 7, July 2016, pp. 8-12

INDEX

IMAGE CREDITS

CHAPTER 1

Figure 1.0	Matthew Jones
Figure 1.1	Matthew Jones
Figure 1.2	Matthew Jones
Figure 1.3	Matthew Jones
Figure 1.4	Matthew Jones

CHAPTER 2

Figure 2.0	Matthew Jones
Figure 2.1.1	Matthew Jones
Figure 2.1.2	Matthew Jones
Figure 2.2.0	Matthew Jones
Figure 2.2.1	Archio
Figure 2.2.2	Archio
Figure 2.2.3	FRENCH + TYE
Figure 2.2.4	Archio
Figure 2.2.5	FRENCH + TYE
Figure 2.2.6	Archio
Figure 2.2.7	Matthew Jones
Figure 2.3.0	Oliver Perrott Photography
Figure 2.3.1	Oliver Perrott Photography
Figure 2.3.2	Dunn Architects
Figure 2.3.3	Dunn Architects
Figure 2.3.4	Oliver Perrott Photography
Figure 2.3.5	Oliver Perrott Photography
Figure 2.3.6	Oliver Perrott Photography
Figure 2.4.0	Ash Sakula
Figure 2.4.1	Ash Sakula
Figure 2.4.2	Peter Cook
Figure 2.4.3	Peter Cook
Figure 2.4.4	Peter Cook
Figure 2.4.5	Ash Sakula
Figure 2.4.6	Ash Sakula
Figure 2.4.7	Ash Sakula
Figure 2.5.0	Pollard Thomas Edwards / Tim Crocker
Figure 2.5.1	Pollard Thomas Edwards
Figure 2.5.2	Pollard Thomas Edwards
Figure 2.5.3	Pollard Thomas Edwards / Tim Crocker
Figure 2.5.4	Pollard Thomas Edwards / Tim Crocker
Figure 2.5.5	Pollard Thomas Edwards / Tim Crocker
Figure 2.5.6	Pollard Thomas Edwards / Tim Crocker
Figure 2.6.0	Witherford Watson Mann
Figure 2.6.1	Witherford Watson Mann
Figure 2.6.2	Witherford Watson Mann
Figure 2.6.3	Witherford Watson Mann
Figure 2.6.4	Witherford Watson Mann
Figure 2.6.5	David Grandorge
Figure 2.6.6	Witherford Watson Mann
Figure 2.6.7	Witherford Watson Mann
Figure 2.6.8	Witherford Watson Mann
Figure 2.7.0	Proctor & Matthew Architects / Tim Crocker
Figure 2.7.1	Proctor & Matthews Architects
Figure 2.7.2	Proctor & Matthew Architects / Tim Crocker
Figure 2.7.3	Proctor & Matthew Architects / Tim Crocker
Figure 2.7.4	Proctor & Matthew Architects / Tim Crocker
Figure 2.7.6	Proctor & Matthew Architects / Tim Crocker
Figure 2.7.5	Proctor and Matthew Architects / Tim Crocker

CHAPTER 3

Figure 3.0	House of Hues, courtesy of The Auckland Project
Figure 3.2.0	Andy Marshall
Figure 3.2.1	Andy Marshall
Figure 3.2.2	Acanthus Clews
Figure 3.2.3	Acanthus Clews
Figure 3.2.4	Andy Marshall
Figure 3.2.5	Acanthus Clews
Figure 3.2.6	Andy Marshall
Figure 3.3.0	GT3 Architects
Figure 3.3.1	GT3 Architects
Figure 3.3.2	GT3 Architects
Figure 3.3.3	GT3 Architects
Figure 3.3.4	GT3 Architects
Figure 3.4.0	SJK Architects
Figure 3.4.1	SJK Architects
Figure 3.4.2	SJK Architects
Figure 3.4.3	SJK Architects
Figure 3.4.4	SJK Architects
Figure 3.4.5	SJK Architects
Figure 3.5.0	Cloud 9 Architectural Photography
Figure 3.5.1	Cloud 9 Architectural Photography
Figure 3.5.2	Cloud 9 Architectural Photography
Figure 3.5.3	Cloud 9 Architectural Photography
Figure 3.5.4	Cloud 9 Architectural Photography
Figure 3.6.0	House of Hues, courtesy of The Auckland Project
Figure 3.6.1	Niall Mclaughlin Architects
Figure 3.6.2	Niall Mclaughlin Architects
Figure 3.6.3	House of Hues, courtesy of The Auckland Project
Figure 3.6.4	Niall Mclaughlin Architects
Figure 3.6.5	Steven Landles, courtesy of The Auckland Project
Figure 3.6.6	Auckland Trust

CHAPTER 4

Figure 4.0	Giulia Vallone
Figure 4.2.0	Neil O'Driscoll
Figure 4.2.1	Studio Weave
Figure 4.2.2	Studio Weave
Figure 4.2.3	Neil O'Driscoll
Figure 4.2.4	Brian Cregan
Figure 4.2.5	Neil O'Driscoll
Figure 4.2.6	Brian Cregan
Figure 4.3.0	Knowsley Council
Figure 4.3.1	Mark Wray Architects
Figure 4.3.2	Mark Wray Architects
Figure 4.3.3	Knowsley Council
Figure 4.3.4	Knowsley Council
Figure 4.3.5	Knowsley Council
Figure 4.3.6	Knowsley Council
Figure 4.4.0	Keith Hunter
Figure 4.4.1	Austin-Smith:Lord
Figure 4.4.2	Austin-Smith:Lord
Figure 4.4.3	Keith Hunter
Figure 4.4.4	Keith Hunter
Figure 4.4.5	Keith Hunter
Figure 4.5.0	Nobu Tanaka / Cork County Council
Figure 4.5.1	Giulia Vallone / Cork County Council
Figure 4.5.2	Cork County Council